MULTISPECIES ASSEMBLIES

EVA MEIJER

CC BY-NC-ND © 2025 by Eva Meijer

This license enables reusers to copy and distribute the material in any medium or format in unadapted form only, for noncommercial purposes only, and only so long as attribution is given to the creator.

CC BY-NC-ND includes the following elements:

BY: credit must be given to the creator.
NC: Only noncommercial uses of the work are permitted.
ND: No derivatives or adaptations of the work are permitted.

This first edition published by:

VINE Press • 158 Massey Road • Springfield, VT 05156 • USA

ISBN: 979-8-9896172-2-7 (paperback) 979-8-9896172-3-4 (e-book)

PHILOSOPHY / Political

NATURE / Animal Rights

POLITICAL SCIENCE / Political Process

CONTENTS

Introduction: The Garden	1
1. Why We Need Multispecies Assemblies	7
2. Outline of the Model of Multispecies Assembly	33
3. The Position of Animals, Plants, Human Youth, Environmental Entities, and Others in Multispecies Assemblies	51
4. Two Examples of Multispecies Assemblies	70
5. Steps Towards Multispecies Assemblies	79
Endnotes	88
Acknowledgments	96

Introduction: The Garden

The garden has a life of its own. When I moved into this house four years ago, all the trees had been cut down, and the grass had been mowed short. My dog companions, Doris and Olli, used the garden to run around, and Olli enjoyed taking naps outside on warm days in the dens he dug for that purpose. But apart from the occasional slug, I saw no other animals in the grass, and the birds stayed away. A month after we moved in, it rained for weeks, and the right side of the garden became a long pool. From inside the house, I looked up trees and plants native to the area. I did some planting in the months that followed, but over time it became clear to me that this had been entirely unnecessary: The roots of the trees that grew in the garden before were still in the ground, and the same was true for the roots of grasses and many other plants. New plants and trees also were planted by the wind, by birds flying overhead, and by trees from the neighboring garden.

I have always lived with nonhuman animals, but I never felt I owned them or was in any way above them hierarchically. If anything, they have been my guardians and teachers and not the other way around. I have specific knowledge and skills relevant to human society while they possess other skills and knowledges. I feel similarly about the garden, clearly an entity of its own and one that now, after four years, has many inhabitants. After the trees grew back, the birds came. Sparrows and blue tits rest and eat in the black alders. Wood pigeons eat the berries from the elderberry tree. Starlings raid the currant bush. Many bees and other insects visit early in the year, after the wild geraniums and dandelions have flowered. There are quite a lot of ant hills, with more developing every few months. In the summer, I can count seven different varieties of grass. Frogs, toads, and salamanders live in the wet parts toward the back of the garden. Different species of mice live in and underneath the shed. Bats visit.

Over the past few years, several of my neighbors have offered me their old lawnmowers after they bought new ones. There is nothing spectacular about this garden in the eyes of most humans. It looks quite wild and not very beautiful to them, nor is it very large. But it is now a home to many beings, and its transformation feels spectacular to me. I recognize only a small percentage of the insects I encounter when I sit outside on a sunny afternoon. Last summer, the trees were finally tall enough to provide shade, which made the garden a refuge during hot days.

For me, the garden came with an obligation to care for its inhabitants and intervene when necessary and a responsibility to treat it with respect. The former relates to the practical fact that we live near other humans. I must trim the front of the hedge on the side of the street so that neighbors can use the sidewalk and we can live in harmony. But I also feel a more general responsibility toward nonhumans under the current conditions of anthropocentric domination. I will care for any animal I encounter who is injured or sick, so I watch out for the animals in and around the garden. A few injured birds have ended up there.

The responsibility to treat the garden with respect means that I need to have basic knowledge about what goes on there, concerning who lives where and who needs what. I sometimes want to sit outside, but I do not want to harm the smaller animals, so I need to know where they live. Olli, my older dog, used the garden a lot when he was ill, and he did the same – he always walked very carefully, even moving out of the way for slugs. Toads, frogs, and salamanders hibernate in the bushes, and the hedgehog does too, so I should avoid moving fallen leaves and branches in autumn and winter. In general, I feel that I am a guest in the garden. At the same time, I am part of the community it holds together, albeit in a more distant way than the creatures who live in the garden.

For me, treating the garden with respect and caring for nonhumans is both an ethical duty and a political project. In the garden live different communities and individuals, such as the ants in their ant hills and the hedgehog in the heap of dead wood near the fence. The willows and black alder trees are a home for birds and also have their own social systems (the willows in this garden and the one next door are connected through their roots).

Cohabiting raises questions of power and justice, such as property and rights. While I do not see the land as mine, or as human property, other humans do. As a human, I have rights that protect me from other humans. Others living in the garden do not. My encounters with the beings in the garden take place within a larger society that disregards the lives of nonhumans and harms them in very large numbers. Taking seriously nonhuman ways of being and contributing to their flourishing is an act of protest in a society in which animals continue to be exploited by intensive animal farming operations, in test laboratories, and for many entertainment industries, and in which the soil is exhausted through monoculture farming and extraction. On the local level, anthropocentric domination also influences the lives of my nonhuman neighbors. Most gardens in this town are tiled, which makes it difficult for insects and birds to survive. During the annual toad migration, cars and buses kill many frogs, toads, and salamanders. Fishing is a popular hobby of human neighbors.

Using a political lens to look at relations between humans and nonhumans raises many questions about power, justice, political participation, representation of nonhumans, and the formation of new communities. Because more-than-human creatures exercise agency and have their own perspectives on life and relations with humans, it is not enough to simply include their interests in existing human decision-making systems. They should be able to have a say in what happens too. For the garden, this implies that when I need to decide about mowing, planting, organizing activities, or the arrival of new inhabitants, I should consult the inhabitants of the garden. While I now refrain from intervening as much as possible and consider the perspectives of the others before I act when I do intervene, it would be more just if I asked them about their position. The question is: How?

In this essay, I outline a model of political multispecies decision-making based on human models of direct democracy: the multispecies assembly. This model, which I will describe in more detail in chapters two and three, is a form of direct democracy in which humans and more-than-human beings, such as nonhuman animals and plants, discuss questions of shared importance and make political decisions. In multispecies assemblies, beings of different species may speak for themselves or for their communities or, when this is not possible or desirable, are represented by others. The model is non-anthropocentric and non-hierarchical. Under the current circumstances, humans will have to take the initiative to establish assemblies because of human domination. Still, with time, multispecies cultural and political knowledge will emerge, decreasing their role.

Given the omnipresence of anthropocentric domination, setting up multispecies assemblies may seem far-fetched. Viewing relations with other beings as political also may seem outlandish. However, these political relations already exist. Even though most human societies do not recognize this, nonhumans are not passive or voiceless but instead actively co-create these political relations through their cooperation, resistance, and/or refusal. Humans do not exist in a vacuum. Human political agency is formed through engagement with nonhuman forces and is always relational. In a time when human domination of others is nearly all-pervasive, learning to listen to others and interact with them in better ways is an urgent responsibility.

Developing a model of multispecies assembly requires experimentation. Although relations do exist, and the agency of nonhuman others has been increasingly recognized in both theory and practice, it would not be possible to map the full spectrum of relations or outline a full political theory of multispecies assembly at this point. This is because it would be empirically impossible and also because new political models need to be developed from the ground up, incorporating the perspectives of other beings in the process. While I can outline the features of a model of multispecies assembly, its actual functioning will only become apparent in practice, through the engagement of human and nonhuman agents.

Here, I should also recognize my limitations as a human who is situated in a specific way: I am incapable of speaking for all others, and I do not feel authorized to do so. Furthermore, we cannot fully know what happens once humans begin to interact differently with other-than-human beings in assemblies. As Hannah Arendt writes, something new and unpredictable comes into being when those who are different meet in a common space and enter political engagement.

Because humans are not used to listening to nonhumans politically or seeing them as political beings, developing a model of multispecies democracy requires new practices of multispecies knowledge creation. New methods of deliberation and decision-making need to be developed in assemblies. What humans view as 'political' and 'political agency' will probably change in this process because different beings have their own perspectives on the community and democratic interaction. This will lead to new democratic challenges. But it also offers hope. Humans can learn from other beings how to live more peacefully alongside those who are different, live more sustainably on this planet, and foster what matters for all of us.

1

WHY WE NEED MULTISPECIES ASSEMBLIES

For a long time, concepts such as political agency, justice, and membership in the political community were regarded in Western philosophy and modern nation-states as exclusively human territory. Nonhumans, and many humans too, were seen as lacking the capacities to be part of the political realm and thus excluded from democratic decision-making (and in many cases from the moral community as well). In recent years, this idea has been challenged from different directions. Philosophers such as Martha Nussbaum,[1] and Sue Donaldson and Will Kymlicka,[2] draw on insights from animal rights theory and political philosophy to argue that, like human animals, nonhuman animals also deserve justice. Ecofeminists like Carol Adams and Lori Gruen have shown that the oppression of women, animals, and nature are related.[3] Jane Bennett[4] and other new materialists have pointed out that human existence is always affected and constituted by nonhuman forces and that human bodies are already more than human. Scholars in critical plant studies propose viewing plants as beings with interests that should be considered ethically and politically.[5] These ideas are not new: Alternatives to anthropocentric theorizing exist in non-western ontologies and epistemologies,[6] as I will discuss in more detail later.

Viewing nonhuman beings such as oaks, flies, dogs, and mountains as subjects of political theorizing is a critical project that asks us to describe patterns of exclusion and injustice, to map structures of domination of nonhumans, and to compare these with structures of domination of humans. It also asks us to challenge hierarchies that may seem normal and natural because they are ingrained in our thinking and practices. But analyzing and describing injustices in this way is not enough: We need to articulate alternatives as well. To develop these alternatives, we need new forms of engaging with nonhuman others.

If we focus solely on including the interests of nonhuman others, like animals and plants, in existing political institutions and practices, representing them as if they were humans and determining what is the good life for them, then we risk repeating anthropocentrism and human dominance. This is because humans would still be deciding what happens – often based on flawed knowledge due to historical and ongoing bias in research. Furthermore, mechanisms of human domination over other beings include silencing them, devaluing their knowledge structures, making their labor for humans and ecosystems invisible, and other practices that deny and 'background' their agency.[7] So, change must begin with more-than-human beings. This does not mean we need to start from scratch. Existing institutions, practices, and concepts will be essential in reformulating relations and building new life-worlds. However, they must be further developed to fit the multispecies context through engagement with other beings.

Current forms of representative democracy are not well-suited for fishes, cows, or forests, nor for young human children. A well-functioning model of multispecies political deliberation and decision-making must be tied to a specific place and based on direct interaction. Existing political systems have undemocratic aspects concerning human citizens, too. For example, industry (and capitalism more broadly) have too much influence on political decision-making, as can clearly be seen in the case of the climate crisis. The political structure also tends to silence marginalized people. There are, however, alternatives for democratic decision-making, of which the assembly is the most promising concerning the more-than-human world.

Assemblies in the Anthropocene

Assemblies are an ancient model for political decision-making. In ancient Greece, assemblies took place in city-states and were called *ecclesia*. Citizens would gather on a hill, at a market square, or in an amphitheater or other specifically designed building to discuss and decide upon matters of common concern. However, this form of government is not specifically European. As David Graeber describes in *Fragments of an Anarchist Anthropology*, many non-western communities around the world that governed and continue to govern themselves by exercising direct democracy use assemblies to deliberate, either because they always did so or in response to state oppression. Assemblies are also not necessarily tied to citizenship, which is an exclusionary category, as the example of the ancient Greeks already shows.

In fact, there are many different models of assembly. Some include all members of the community, while others include only a selection of them; some have legislative power, while others only inform the government; some are the main form of government in a community, while others constitute only one small part of a larger chain of decision-making. In the climate crisis and related ecological crises, citizens' assemblies are currently regarded as a promising democratic tool by activists and policy-makers. Both citizens' assemblies and popular assemblies, like the *ecclesia*, contain elements that are important for thinking about multispecies assemblies. I will outline their characteristics briefly.

Citizens' assemblies can take different forms, but they share characteristics. They generally select their members through a two-stage process called sortition to form a representative cross-section of the public. Members of the assembly are then given information and time to develop an informed opinion on the subject matter at stake, coming to a collective standpoint through a deliberative process. Assemblies usually have between 50 and 200 members. Their advice is generally not binding. They often provide recommendations to politicians or the general public and might exert indirect influence on agenda-setting or policy-making.[8]

In contrast, popular assemblies are a form of direct democracy in which citizens, residents, or other groups (such as workers) gather to discuss and decide upon issues of collective importance. Decisions can be made through consensus or voting. Popular assemblies can fill different roles for a government. In ancient Greece, the *ecclesia* was the government. Some contemporary assemblies explicitly aim to provide an alternative to the state, such as the Zapatistas in Rebel Zapatista Autonomous Municipalities.[9] Anarchist communities do too. For example, different forms of non-hierarchical collective government were tried out during the Occupy Movement. Other models of popular assembly are part of a larger political structure in nation-states. For example, in New England, the town meeting, in which all community members can decide upon matters of common concern, is a traditional part of local government.

Assemblies are already used for decision-making about nature and the more-than-human world. In the context of the climate crisis, citizens' assemblies are increasingly considered to be an important ecopolitical tool for progress.[10] On their website, the environmental movement Extinction Rebellion lists its Third Demand as a Citizens' Assembly on Climate and Ecological Justice. This is their most important demand because "it gives people from different walks of life a seat at the table, and places the power to transform our world in their hands."[11] They are not the only ones who connect democratic decision-making about the climate and other ecological issues to citizens' assemblies. The citizens' assembly model is currently called upon internationally to include citizens in political decision-making, discussions of complex questions regarding policies in detail, and the creation of better governance processes that can enhance citizens' trust in institutions.

Extinction Rebellion does not call for democratic reform because, according to their website, this would take too long to realize. It would require constitutional change, which is a lengthy democratic process if it would be realizable at all. However, democratic reform is essential for more sustainable and just societies. Ecopolitical problems like the climate crisis, loss of biodiversity, and the accelerating extinction of species are challenging to solve in the context of neoliberal nation-states. Existing political institutions and processes are typically unsuitable for addressing the climate crisis and related ecological crises because of the focus on the short term that election cycles bring. Other reasons to turn to assemblies include the gap between the people and political decision-making/politicians as well as the lack of inclusion and representation of groups who arguably have the most to lose, such as human youth and nonhuman animals. Citizens' assemblies are more than models for facilitating political decision-making. There is a radical side to them, which lies in their capacity to find new solutions for ecopolitical questions and to foster social change.[12] Therefore, citizens' assemblies show glimpses of an alternative to nation-state models and hold a democratic promise which is lost in current representative models of democracy.

Some communities using popular assembly to make decisions also take the more-than-human world seriously, such as eco-anarchist groups or the Zapatistas, who explicitly aim to create an ecological society, which includes setting up projects for environmental protection and restoration of the land and forests. However, all assemblies are currently made up of humans.

Who can become a part of an assembly has changed throughout history, and it differs between human cultures. In ancient Greece, only citizens – free males – were allowed to join. In the town meetings of New England, all citizens of the community are welcome.[13] Citizens' assemblies comprise a selection of human citizens (sometimes including human youth). In the Rebel Zapatista Autonomous Municipalities, political decisions are made by all human residents above the age of twelve. While there have been experiments in representing future generations in assemblies, and some do aim to represent nature, the fact that humans are the ones who decide is never challenged. This is problematic from the perspective of justice and democracy, as I will explain in more detail below. Epistemically it is also a missed opportunity, especially regarding ecological and social decision-making. Other animals, trees, and other plants have their own knowledge of our shared world, and humans could learn from those perspectives. Taking more perspectives into account sketches a richer picture of life and offers new opportunities for acting and thinking.

We therefore need an account of *multispecies* assembly, in which different beings come together to discuss and decide upon matters of shared concern, and where those who cannot be present but are affected by decision-making are represented by others. Elements of citizens' assembly and popular assembly can help to construct the basis of a model of multispecies assembly. But there will also be significant differences regarding language, embodied political interaction, decision-making, scope, and scale of the assembly, as I will discuss in more detail in the next chapter.

The *Multispecies* in Multispecies Assembly

The critical reader might object that it is neither possible nor necessary to develop multispecies assemblies or forms of multispecies politics and government more broadly. Humans in anthropocentric societies often believe that other-than-human beings lack the skills required for deliberation, making it impossible for them to participate in assemblies. Furthermore, there are significant differences between animals, plants, human youth, and environmental entities with regard to their capacities, forms of expression and interests, and their relations to human political societies, making it difficult, if not impossible, to form assemblies that include all of them. Humans might also doubt the necessity of allowing other-than-human beings to speak for themselves, because they think humans are best suited to represent other beings. Instead of entering messy processes of living differently, they may believe that it would be better to measure the interests of others and develop a fair system of representation, not only because this would be easier for humans, but also because this would better benefit nonhumans. However, developing new forms of multispecies politics from a human perspective would not necessarily be easier. It also would not be just.

The view that only humans are capable of conversations and political deliberation seems natural and necessary to many humans because there is a general assumption in Western cultures that more-than-human beings do not speak. However, this belief is both the cause and result of silencing processes in these societies. Through practices of subordination and violence, humans physically silence other beings. Culturally or symbolically, anthropocentric ideologies leave little room for other-than-human voices to be heard. This position is not neutral or natural. Alternatives may be found in certain non-western and Indigenous cosmologies that recognize the value of other-than-human perspectives. In other words, the idea that nonhuman beings are either silent or have nothing of value to say is a Western anthropocentric viewpoint that does not reflect reality. Many animal species and communities have languages and also communicate with members of other species[14]. Plants have complex communication systems as well as intricate forms of cognition and community about which we do not yet know much. Fungi use electrical signals to communicate with each other and with plants.[15] Ongoing biological and ethological research into the languages, cultures, and capacities of more-than-human beings challenges us to rethink our relations with them. Rethinking relations includes rethinking the figure of the human, because ideas about what it means to be human have been formed in contraposition to false ideas about nonhumans.

Doubting if nonhumans speak, if multispecies communication is possible, and if we can understand nonhuman others can be an expression of what I have elsewhere termed *species skepticism*.[16] Species skepticism refers to the position that, while language allows us to get an idea of what other humans think, the minds of other animals (and perhaps other beings capable of language, like plants) must be a mystery to us. This is a speciesist variation of skepticism about knowing others,[17] which is often connected to the idea that only *human* language is actual language.

However, this position is flawed. We do not learn to understand others by rationally grasping their position through language but rather through embodied encounters in which different forms of expression factor. Meaning is created through learning, attention, habit formation, and other ways. (For example, art can help us understand something different about life than argumentation and language through images or sensory experiences.) Species is only one factor in constructing meaning with others and in getting to know someone else. Species-specific characteristics shape how different beings communicate and understand one another, but material, social, economic, historical, and cultural relations also matter. Street dogs have different forms of sociality than domesticated dogs who share households with humans and perhaps other animals. Humans who live in forests understand trees differently than people who live in cities and, therefore, have different forms of co-creating meaning with trees.

Species skepticism is sticky in anthropocentric culture. It can be hard to overcome because it obstructs getting to know others and taking them seriously. If you assume someone has nothing to say, you will not be curious about their life or ask them questions, thereby limiting possible interaction. But when we encounter other beings as fellow creatures who have something to say to us, we can begin a new conversation.

Multispecies conversations already exist, for example, between companion animals and their humans, foresters and trees, or nature writers and environmental entities. Even in anthropocentric societies, there is often a basic understanding of what is beneficial for many animal and plant beings and what harms them. Furthermore, humans are not the only ones who are involved in processes of getting to know others. Other beings, especially nonhuman animals, pay close attention to humans and know them well. (Many animals need to do so to avoid violence or death. Perhaps they will ignore humans when they finally can.) So, while we need to learn to interact differently with nonhumans on a political and cultural level, there are many existing practices that we can draw on to learn how to do so.

Another objection to multispecies assemblies could be that it would be more feasible and just to develop assemblies with only one category of beings (e.g., domesticated animals, ash trees, or human youth). This could be more feasible because setting up assemblies with only one nonhuman group would require less new knowledge or bring more focus. However, knowing how to act toward one individual or a community often involves consideration of the whole system of relations, including connections between different beings.

Developing assemblies with only one nonhuman species or one category of beings could be considered more just because human ethical and political duties might weigh more heavily toward some beings than toward others. An example of this view is found in the work of Donaldson and Kymlicka, who argue that because of historical and current relations, humans have more substantial duties toward domesticated animals than toward wild animals, which influences what kind of political relations we can, but also should have with these beings.[18] Similarly, philosopher Clare Palmer argues that humans have stronger duties toward the animals who are most affected by human acts than to others.[19]

While humans may have stronger duties toward certain animals than toward other animals, or stronger duties toward nonhuman animals than plants, or stronger duties toward plants than environmental entities like rivers, the problem with this line of reasoning in setting up assemblies is that the choices that are made in a given space will likely affect all beings who reside in the area. Hence, their interests need to be included in the decision-making for reasons of justice. Wild animals and plants may suffer if humans and domesticated animals determine what happens and consider only their own interests. Furthermore, when more-than-human beings experience more freedom, relations will change. This is especially likely for more-than-human animals, who might choose to leave human society or set up new arrangements for themselves, which will likely change the position of both domesticated and wild animals in relation to human society. A more general objection to single-group assemblies is that they would be undemocratic because they would be exclusionary. In existing liberal democracies, the starting point is a *demos* of humans. If we instead take a given physical space as the starting point for politics, who is part of the *demos* changes. So, while relations do matter, and human duties do vary, these differences are problems that must be solved in assemblies of which all beings are a part. From a pragmatic point of view, and for reasons of justice, it is therefore necessary to include all who are affected. Of course, assemblies do not always have to consist of many different groups or agents; perhaps humans should sometimes form assemblies focused on only one group for some particular purpose.

Including all who are affected in assemblies raises two further complexities: firstly, the problem of opposing interests, and secondly, the degree to which this model may be very demanding for humans, who will need to give up their self-proclaimed rights to the land and the bodies and labor of other beings, which will profoundly affect their ways of living. I will discuss both points in more detail in the next chapter. Here, I want to note that there is a tendency to overemphasize struggle in political philosophy and public debate. We currently live in a time of ecological disaster in which the interests of many beings are similar: All living creatures rely on the health of the natural environment, and we all need better structures of care. Human interests are not opposed to those of other beings.

Multispecies Justice

In 'multispecies justice theory,' we find a clear articulation of the idea that we must take the interconnections between humans and other beings into account when conceptualizing just ways forward.[20] Multispecies justice theory is an eco-relational approach to justice that goes beyond dichotomies such as human/animal, living/nonliving, and nature/culture to develop new forms of living with others (including nonhuman animals, plants, ecosystems, ancestors, future generations, and nonliving matter). Scholars such as Danielle Celermajer and Christine Winter argue that de-centering the human and reconceptualizing the scope of justice is necessary for developing an alternative to the ongoing ecological violence in the Anthropocene resulting from human supremacy. They connect human justice to nonhuman justice in different ways.

The first thing to note when rethinking the scope of justice is that human exceptionalism is harmful to humans because at the center of this ideology lies an image of the human that was constructed through racist and capitalist modes of being. Anthropocentric ideologies have excluded and harmed, and continue to hurt, many marginalized peoples. This mechanism of exclusion has recently been termed 'hierarchical anthropocentrism' by scholars such as Dinesh Wadiwel.[21] Hierarchical anthropocentrism also leads to material inequality, which is clearly visible concerning the climate crisis. Rich humans in western parts of the world contribute most to this crisis, while poor communities are most affected; at the same time, the rich are in the best position to make the necessary changes to survive. Hierarchical anthropocentrism is not just bad for humans; it also leads to violence against many other beings, such as nonhuman animals and plants, and the ecosystems on which the health of all living beings relies. Their interests and lives matter too. Furthermore, we cannot position humans outside of the natural realm: Human agency and subjectivity are always influenced and shaped by the agency of others, including nonhumans and social structures. Here, it is again important to recognize that alternatives already exist. In different Indigenous traditions we already find multispecies alternatives to anthropocentric accounts of justice and politics.[22]

Extending justice to nonhuman beings and entities and focusing on creating better relations instead of weighing existing interests can provide an alternative to human-centered models of politics. Such an alternative is needed to counter the ecological collapse that characterizes our time and to address large-scale violence toward others. There probably will not be a revolution leading us from anthropocentric neoliberalism to multispecies justice, but rather a slow transformation. Multispecies assemblies can inform this transformation because they include the voices and perspectives of nonhumans, which should be foregrounded in developing any new forms of politics. This leads us to the questions of multispecies political participation, representation, and voice.

Political Participation and Representation

Many existing political practices and institutions are unsuitable for multispecies deliberation and decision-making because they rely on human language or human cognition, require the ability to read or hold a pencil, or take place in spaces that are not accessible or comfortable for other-than-human beings. This does not mean that there is no political engagement between humans and nonhumans, and it also does not mean that human political practices and institutions cannot be extended to incorporate the voices and agencies of others. There are already different proposals for considering the perspectives and voices of nonhumans in political decision-making processes.

Philosopher and sociologist Bruno Latour, for example, argues for a 'parliament of things.'[23] According to Latour, humans are always part of networks with other *actants*[24], human and nonhuman, in which beings affect one another and co-constitute situations. He also believes that traditional divisions such as nature versus culture and science versus politics are unsuitable for understanding and describing reality. The exclusion of more-than-human beings from political decision-making is based on a false picture of reality because it presents humans as separate from the rest, leading to bad eco-political results. Latour writes that we need a parliament of things in which nonhuman interests are also brought to the table. However, in Latour's scenario, humans do the political speaking and decision-making, even though they are constantly influenced by others.

The same is true for the *Rights of Nature* movement, the second example of more-than-human politics I want to discuss. Rights of nature currently receive much attention in academia and public discourse and are sometimes presented as a response to the climate crisis and related ecological crises. While the term 'rights' connects to a Western framework of constitutions, courtrooms, and UN declarations, rights of nature are often rooted in the cosmologies of Indigenous peoples and institutionalized through the efforts of Indigenous activists. This is, for example, visible in the way rights of nature, or rather, *pachamama*, are anchored in Ecuador's constitutional law. The Montechristi Constitution of 2008 recognizes nature as the holder of inalienable rights. It describes Ecuador as a "plurinational and interethnic state" in which ecosystems like forests, mountains, rivers, seas, and communities of animals living there are all legal subjects. This change in the law was driven by the Indigenous movement, which sprang from Indigenous uprisings in the 1990s, and by insights from environmental sciences, activism, and advocacy.[25] The Montechristi Constitution connects an Indigenous understanding of rights to a Western concept and makes it possible for people to go to court on behalf of nature.[26] Another example is New Zealand's Whanganui River, which was recently granted personhood after 140 years of struggle for its recognition as an ancestor by the local Māori tribe of Whanganui in the North Island.[27]

While it seems promising to use rights to protect natural entities and promote respect for these entities in human societies, there are also dangers connected to this approach. Scholars such as Mihnea Tanasescu show that the rights of nature discourse sometimes repeats colonialist attitudes.[28] There is also a lack of clarity and consensus around what 'nature' means in legal and political arrangements. Furthermore, the discourse about the rights of nature is sometimes anthropocentric in various ways. For example, 'animals' are usually not mentioned in rights of nature discourse or laws, and rights of nature are often framed as important only insofar as they promote the future welfare of humans. Because rights are a human construct and are always embedded in larger systems built on human supremacy,[29] arguing for rights of nature risks reinforcing the anthropocentrism that activists and scholars aim to challenge.

An alternative position can be found in animal political philosophy, where scholars such as Clemens Driessen[30] and myself[31] propose that we view human-nonhuman animal communication as deliberation. For example, I discuss goose-human deliberation in the context of conflicts about habitats, dog-human deliberation concerning the dog leash, and human-mouse deliberation concerning spatial interaction and sharing habitats. Sue Donaldson also discusses forms of multispecies deliberation concerning public space.[32] She emphasizes the role of material interventions in deliberation between humans and other animals, such as changes in a landscape. Donaldson also stresses the importance of focusing on embodied interactive processes instead of single decision-making moments. While these proposals for approaching human-nonhuman animal deliberation offer many clues for incorporating animal voices in multispecies assemblies, they only focus on one – albeit extremely heterogeneous – group: nonhuman animals.

All three examples offer insights into what matters in multispecies politics but only solve part of the puzzle. Latour rightly argues against binary understandings of politics/science and nature/culture and also rightly emphasizes the interconnectedness of different forms of agency and the need for representation of nonhumans. However, his model is too human-centered and glosses over the fact that communication is possible with many nonhumans. Another problem is that in describing political decision-making, Latour's model groups together all nonhumans, obscuring important differences concerning social relations and capacities that should shape how we set up a parliament. Val Plumwood notes that 'terms like "nature" lump seals and elephants along with mountains and clouds.'[33] Latour adds pencils and automobiles to the mix.

Similar objections arise in the case of the rights of nature movement: Representation of nonhumans by humans is not enough because nonhuman voices also need to be taken into account. For a mountain, self-representation might not matter, but for many animals it does. While rights can be a tool in working toward multispecies politics, it is crucial to be critical of their anthropocentric content and history and to be attentive to the voices of other-than-human beings.

Work in animal philosophy that focuses on these voices by taking animal and multispecies deliberation seriously can inform interaction with nonhuman animals in multispecies assemblies. However, focusing solely on more-than-human animals is not enough. The model of multispecies assembly should also incorporate the voices and interests of other beings, such as plants, and this will require other forms of interaction and representation.

Taking the Voices of Others into Account

Before discussing some examples of multispecies government in practice, I must elaborate briefly on what I mean by 'the voices of nonhumans.' The concepts of 'voice' and 'political voice' have different meanings for humans, other animals, plants, and environmental entities. They may also mean something different within these categories of beings, resulting from species differences, social differences, and other factors that determine how we express ourselves, what kinds of questions are discussed collectively, what kinds of communication are possible, and how those who speak should be heard. These differences matter for the political participation and representation of nonhumans. Furthermore, 'political voice' does not refer to one practice but rather to a collection of practices that share a family resemblance. As Ludwig

Wittgenstein writes, concepts do not have one universal, fixed meaning that we can determine by philosophizing. Instead, their meaning changes in different contexts, depending on how they are used, the 'grammar' of the situation, and other factors. To study a concept, we should consider the language-game in which it is embedded.[34] This is an ongoing process because there will always be hidden and new language-games.

In the case of humans, 'political voice' can refer to official political standing. When women got the vote, they had more of a political voice than before. The concept can also refer to counter-practices: People can make their voices be heard in protests on the streets and online. Or in assemblies. Not all instances of 'voice' include an actual voice or language: Taking part in demonstrations, practicing refusal, or being represented are all examples of situations in which beings may not actually speak but do have voice. At the same time, structural processes of silencing take away the political voice of some groups of humans.

If we extend this view of political voice to other animals, other practices come to light. Animals can act in response to human political structures: They might refuse, protest, or consent to be represented. Animals also may have their own species-specific or cultural ways of voting, diplomacy, and democracy that express their political voices in their own communities or between communities. There can be interspecies or multispecies practices in which humans and other animals explore or practice new forms of democracy, in which they can help develop a better understanding of the voices of the others with whom they interact.

Extending the multispecies assembly model to plants and forests may seem far-fetched in Western knowledge paradigms but not in different Indigenous practices. Leanne Betasamosake Simpson, for example, writes about international relations between human and nonhuman communities that have their own forms of agency.[35] Robin Wall Kimmerer discusses how viewing plants as 'plant beings' changes relations and emphasizes the importance of listening to plants.[36] This is a plea shared by critical plant studies scholars.[37] 'Voice' in this context refers not only to the symbolic standing of these beings but also to how they behave and express themselves.

In these examples of the uses of 'political voice,' language and politics are intertwined. Our current understanding of the concept and its possible meanings will likely change shape once humans begin to listen to nonhumans politically. This is because what nonhuman beings want and say will have more weight. New forms of political voice will probably come into being. These may resemble existing forms in the same way that animals (including humans) in sanctuaries adapt their modes of expression and learn to understand others in the context of a new community. Humans probably will find instances of political voice where they never expected them.

Examples of Multispecies Co-Government

The idea of multispecies assemblies is not just a utopian fantasy. While official multispecies assemblies do not exist, as far as I am aware, there are many examples of practices in which humans consult other beings politically, actively form communities with them, and strive for multispecies justice. These include practices that display how some humans do not see themselves as outside of the rest of the living world, which affects all decisions that are made.

Multispecies Cosmologies

The number of humans who do not see themselves as outside of the rest of nature and who approach politics and justice from a multispecies perspective is larger than those in the Western world might assume. Philosopher Christine Winter writes about Mātauranga Māori theory and practice as a way of enacting multispecies justice.[38] She reminds us that 'multispecies justice' is far from a new concept and urges scholars to mention and learn from non-western thought. She discusses Mātauranga Māori concepts that express the interconnectedness of all beings, such as *manaatikanga* (practices of providing support, care, hospitality, and generosity and showing respect for others) and *whanaungatanga* (connectedness to self, family and others, places, and the multispecies realm secured through relationships). According to Winter, these concepts can guide the development of multispecies justice theory by showing that a different way of living as humans already exists.

Other non-western traditions of thought and practice offer alternatives to anthropocentric ontology. For example, in Daoism, certain key concepts like *dao* (the way, which refers to living in line with the way of life), *ziran* (naturalness, spontaneity, or 'so of itself'), *wuwei* (acting through not acting, philosophically often understood as responsive attunement) and *wanwu*, or the ten thousand things (everything that is there in the universe) express an attitude toward life that is based on entanglements instead of binary oppositions, and that understands the universe as plural and constantly moving. Daoism locates humans in an immense and ever-evolving web of beings. In this web, humans are not hierarchically above other beings or things, and to live a good life is to live in line with the motion of life, which requires attentiveness to others.

While these examples of non-western multispecies theorizing do not include the kind of multispecies deliberation and representation I discuss below, they do show an alternative to Western anthropocentric models of (political or other) decision-making. They also offer another perspective on what it means to live rightly with other beings in a world that is not mute.

Multispecies Cultures

Importantly, nonhuman animals also have cultural practices that should be considered when we discuss non-anthropocentric forms of politics, community, and decision-making. As with language, animal cultures are currently a focus of research within science. New studies appear regularly, showing that cultural practices exist not only in elephant, whale, and bonobo communities but also in communities of songbirds, bees, and many others.[39] What anthropologist Arturo Escobar calls the 'pluriverse'[40] – the many worlds with their own forms of knowledge and practices that make up our universe – is inherently multispecies. Nonhuman animal forms of knowledge-creation and expression sometimes differ from human cosmologies, but many animal traditions, habits, and practices resemble those of humans.

In addition to single-species cultures and life-worlds, there are also multispecies cultures and shared life-worlds of which humans might be a part. Humans often view human society as a human project. But, animals who are part of human communities, such as domesticated animals, have co-shaped these communities and human cultures more generally. This co-shaping occurs partly through indirect influence: Humans who live with other animals, watch them, and think about them are affected by them. Communities are also co-formed through direct influence, as in the acts and expressions of other animals. The fact that we already have this cultural multispecies experience supports the idea that certain nonhuman animals can speak for themselves in assemblies: We already understand one another and are comfortable with sharing space. Those animals who are less comfortable with close proximity to humans might change their position when they are not harmed by humans anymore. It is also possible to interact with more distance through spatial and material interventions.

There are already spaces in which humans and other animals actively collaborate to form new communities and to create common forms of decision-making. These experiments in living mostly take place in animal sanctuaries, where humans aim to live with other animals on the basis of equality and care instead of domination. Some sanctuaries have already developed practices that can inspire and inform how humans should engage with other animals in assemblies. A good example is VINE Sanctuary, in which the humans understand themselves not as governing other animals but as part of a multispecies community.[41] The animal members of the sanctuary community not only participate in predetermined activities but also are consulted when decisions are made about their lives or the course of the community. Through learning and experimentation, the humans at VINE develop a better understanding of what multispecies government can and should be. Over time, they become more attuned to the desires and opinions of others. Learning about animals' opinions, preferences, and perspectives can be done by giving them options concerning where to live and with whom, what to eat, what kind of activities to participate in, and the extent of interaction with humans.

The animal residents at VINE shape this process and how the community evolves. One way they do this is by choosing roles for themselves in the community.[42] For example, some residents take on the role of guardian, like roosters who keep an eye out for hawks and cows and alpacas who deter foxes and coyotes. Others become teachers, like the cow Coco, who instructed and assisted younger cows who came to the sanctuary without family members to learn from. Taking on roles, or choosing a job, is only one of the ways different individuals shape the community and their own lives.

To learn what the animals mean and want, the humans at the sanctuary strive to pay attention. pattrice jones, who co-founded VINE Sanctuary, describes the importance of empathic imagination in forming new relations with animals outside of human supremacy. In Kathryn Gillespie's book *The Cow with Ear Tag# 1389*, jones also describes the practice of consulting animals when decisions need to be made. Decisions about animals "ought to be made, insofar as possible, in consultation with animals. If that's not possible, the next best thing is to be in physical proximity to animals like those you're thinking about, so that you don't make the mistake of treating them as abstractions."[43]

In addition to sanctuaries, examples of how to live differently and make decisions together with other animals can be found in multispecies auto-ethnography, in which researchers describe their own experiences living with nonhuman animals and centering the animals' perspectives and positions. Ethologist Barbara Smuts, for example, describes how she learned to live with a group of baboons, which meant she had to learn their language.[44] She also writes about learning to live differently with her dog companion, Safi, who took the lead in forming their friendship.

In sanctuaries and multispecies auto-ethnographies, humans often take the initiative to rescue, adopt, and care for animals. However, there are also situations in which other animals decide to support human political acts, like riot dogs. Riot dogs are street dogs who support anarchist activists in their struggle against the police by participating in street demonstrations and riots. One of the most famous riot dogs is Loukanikos. Loukanikos was a street dog who joined the anti-austerity protests in Greece in 2009 and 2010. He was known for his fearlessness. He barked at the police, joined protests and street battles with the police, and became a celebrity; he was nominated as 'Person of the Year' for *Time* magazine. While he was cared for by activists and organizations, Loukanikos preferred to be on the streets, at least until he grew older and was adopted. He died at the age of ten from medical complications following the inhalation of tear gas. Other well-known riot dogs are Kanellos, also from Greece, and Negro Matapacos from Chile, who joined student protests. Riot dogs are described by activists and the media as acting in solidarity with human protesters. They probably want to defend their home – the streets – and perhaps their community if they are part of an activist group. These dogs can clearly express their opinions about topics of common concern and have their own ideas about the cities and streets we share.

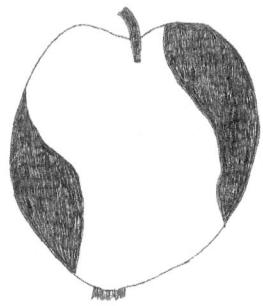

Entangled Agencies

These different examples of multispecies politics offer some clues for understanding the role of humans in assemblies. Human individuals, communities, and cultures are constantly affected by, and in conversation with, human and nonhuman forces, ranging from the weather to their diets, friendships with other animals, language, and even viruses. Acknowledging this offers a different image of what it means to be a subject, a self, or a human than current neoliberal-anthropocentric understandings of the human. At the same time, we are at a point in history in which humans have a strong responsibility toward other beings due to current and past violence. Philosopher Lori Gruen connects both of these elements of human existence—interdependence with others and the responsibility humans have toward nonhumans—in the term 'entangled empathy.'[45] Gruen writes that we are already entangled in relations with others, including other animals. Those relations are now often violent, but we can become more responsive and responsible by practicing caring perception and embodied attunement. Entangled empathy requires more than just a change in attitude; it is a practice in which we learn to live together less violently with others.

For assemblies, responsiveness and responsibility matter, too. Humans have clear responsibilities toward more-than-human others because we are so powerful at this point in time and because the current ways we live with others are almost entirely shaped by human domination. In setting up assemblies, humans need to consider their position toward others. Taking responsibility does not mean intervening more frequently or determining for others what is right for them from behind a laptop or in a courtroom. It means we need to ask these others how they want to live with us and try to find out how we all can co-exist in more just ways, given that our lives are connected. We need to practice responsiveness. Of course, humans have specific skills that matter for and in assemblies, but so do more-than-human animals, plants, fungi, and other beings. Humans in assemblies are just one species among many, all of whom have skills and forms of wisdom.

2

OUTLINE OF THE MODEL OF MULTISPECIES ASSEMBLY

Multispecies assembly is a model of multispecies government that includes the voices and interests of more-than-human animals, plants, human youth, natural entities, future generations, and possibly others. The multispecies assembly model shares features with the popular assembly: Everyone who has an interest in the questions being discussed has a right to speak out and co-decide, and the assembly can provide a democratic (and ecologically just) alternative to current models of government. Like the citizens' assembly, the multispecies assembly requires both education and deliberation.

To overcome human biases and counter the destructive forms of living that are currently the norm, we need to develop this new democratic structure from the ground up by acting and living differently with others. In the multispecies assembly model, the government should not only be more-than-human but also horizontal and non-hierarchical. The model should be attentive to different forms of domination, as total liberation scholars and activists propose, in order not to repeat the oppression it aims to challenge.[46]

Multispecies assemblies can be permanent, as a form of government, or temporary. Assemblies can also be set up to guide the transition from an anthropocentric community to a multispecies community. Temporary assemblies can begin with a question of common interest brought to the attention of others by humans or other animals, after which a group of facilitators map the situation and oversee the assembly. Temporary assemblies can end after a decision has been made and renewed when necessary. Permanent assemblies might meet regularly to deliberate about matters of common concern, similar to how popular assemblies can guide decision-making in anarchist communities. Multispecies assemblies should also include political experiments to find out how best to engage with nonhumans, especially in the transition toward more just communities.

In contrast to human assemblies, which are often not tied to a location and in which human language and deliberation play a vital role, multispecies assemblies are bound to a specific place and environment. In multispecies assemblies, we cannot separate the environment from the beings who participate in assemblies and the questions at stake. The methods of deliberation are based on embodied and situated interaction, as I will discuss in more detail below. Furthermore, in multispecies assemblies, the decision-making process might be more important than the outcome, while human assemblies generally focus on a set outcome.

In their day-to-day set-up, multispecies assemblies should avoid bureaucracy as much as possible because bureaucracy often excludes animal participation. In terms of content, discussions about fair ways of sharing habitats and other living spaces will be common, as will questions about food. Development, or simply the future, also will be an important topic of concern. How will we share communal habitats? How shall we develop social structures in common life-worlds? What structures of care, work, and education will be needed?

All of these, and more, may be topics taken up by multispecies assemblies.

How multispecies assemblies evolve will depend on the precise eco-cultural context. Assemblies might look very different in different places and with different contributors. But as a government structure, they could provide an alternative to the nation-state, perhaps similar to the Zapatistas' reformulation of government, education, healthcare, and other institutions based on Indigenous practice and anarchist insights.

In what follows, I will sketch the model of multispecies assembly and elaborate on how it works in relation to different kinds of beings. I focus on the beginning, not on the end. Whether assemblies should ultimately be institutionalized through a form of anarcho-federalism or take a very different form is a question that can be answered only after assemblies have taken place. However, connections and relations between multispecies assemblies will exist. While assemblies are rooted in specific locations and meetings will occur locally – in a town square, a garden, or a forest – there can be larger assemblies, too. For example, assemblies can be formed around a region or even larger areas where inhabitants are connected through a multispecies culture, traditions, or practices. Assemblies that are far apart geographically may be similar due to being located in similar ecosystems, made up of similar beings, or discussing similar questions. Similar assemblies can cooperate in building knowledge. Because multispecies assemblies should be developed from the ground up, the precise way these connections and possible overlapping forms of government will take shape will have to follow from the new practices developed together with other beings.

Before I sketch the model itself, I will discuss some of the elements of multispecies assemblies in more detail. I focus on duration; experiment, learning, play, and practice-based research; imagination; initiative; knowledge; language and communication; listening; meetings; movement and process; respect for the dignity and flourishing of others; rituals and habits; scale; scope; place; and time. These are not the only ingredients of multispecies assemblies, but they show similarities and differences with anthropocentric assemblies and sketch what is essential in developing multispecies assemblies.

Elements of Multispecies Assemblies

Duration

The duration of assemblies depends on the questions that need to be discussed and the agents involved. There are roughly two types of multispecies assemblies: ongoing and temporal assemblies. Ongoing assemblies are a form of multispecies government that can hold regular or irregular meetings and involve ongoing processes of knowledge formation and deliberation that may include informal conversations, political experiments, and the development of shared habits and other collective practices. Temporal assemblies function the same, but respond to a singular problem, such as a flood, a question about the development of a shared space, or the integration of newcomers. The borders between temporal and ongoing assemblies are not fixed. Temporal assemblies might change into ongoing assemblies, and ongoing assemblies can change shape or end.

Experiment, Learning, Play, and Practice-Based Research

To be able to develop a democratic model that is future-proof, humans need to learn to see themselves as part of a larger whole and to act accordingly. This learning process requires experiments in living and acting differently. Here, we can learn from anarchist practice, in which the messiness of living differently and committing to experimentation and exploration is not eschewed but embraced. In multispecies assemblies, living differently will demand more effort from humans. Among humans, there is at least an abstract notion of an ideal of equality, which is lacking with regard to nonhumans. Humans have been socialized into anthropocentric thinking, and it takes time to unlearn this ideology. Furthermore, while conversations among humans feel familiar to most humans, most of us lack experience in multispecies deliberation.

Humans involved in multispecies assemblies should therefore invest time in getting to know others through ethical multispecies political experiments based on consent, practice-based research, and multispecies learning, especially during the transition from anthropocentric communities to multispecies communities. Learning can be approached rationally – through reading, speaking with other humans, or attending academic conferences – or in a more embodied and situated way. In the multispecies context, we need both kinds of learning.

To figure out how to best deliberate with and represent others, humans can inform themselves through conversation, reading, and other typical forms of learning. But they should also spend time with the beings involved, for example with the sea, an ant community (ants might be able to speak for themselves in some ways), or a grove of trees. An essential part of learning about and with nonhuman beings is becoming attuned to them through the simple act of paying attention.

Another critical aspect of learning with nonhuman others, such as animals and plants, and human youth too, is to engage in spatial and material dialogues to ask them what they want in a specific situation, such as what their preferences are about eating practices, sleeping places, care, or work. In developing multispecies education for young community members, play can be a way of getting to know one another and setting boundaries. But play can be important for adults too. For beings of all ages, play offers space for trying out different roles, twisting hierarchies, and practicing with different kinds of relations. Like humor, play can inform all learning practices.

Imagination

Imagination is necessary to set up practice-based experiments in ethical living with nonhumans and to take their perspective. While the word 'experiment' might bring to mind vivisection and other nonconsensual forms of research using animals as objects, I mean another kind of experiment: practices in which humans aim to live and communicate differently with nonhuman animals and other more-than-human beings. These already exist. For example, at animal sanctuaries like VINE Sanctuary, which I discussed earlier, the humans actively work toward relations without domination by centering the perspectives of nonhumans. Taking the perspectives of our fellow beings can be easy or hard, depending on the questions and beings involved. The idea is not to erase or overcome differences but to seriously consider someone else's view. Human societies have experience with this in the form of art and stories, and human artists should play a role in further developing political multispecies perspective-taking.[47]

Initiative

The initiative for assemblies can be taken by different beings, human and nonhuman. Adult humans can set up an assembly as part of transitioning from an anthropocentric community to a multispecies community or in response to events requiring temporal assemblies, like natural disasters or other significant events. But human youth or dogs could also notice a problem requiring deliberation that human adults do not see and tell them with words or acts that an assembly is needed. Or a community of elephants or horses might become aware of an ecological problem before humans do and change their behavior so that others notice it; they might even explicitly bring it to the attention of others. In other cases, nonhumans might unintentionally signal the need for an assembly through their behavior or appearance, as when plants do not flourish or a river changes color. Humans need to pick up on these changes and can take them as the starting point for an assembly. As assemblies evolve, humans will become more attuned to others and better able to recognize their forms of expression. This may change ideas about and possibilities for taking the initiative for assemblies.

Knowledge

Theorists of deliberation like Iris Young or Jürgen Habermas argue that informed discussions lead to better, more just, and more democratic political decisions than, for example, voting. Through exchanging arguments and perspectives, something extra happens, something more than the calculation of interests. Humans get to know one another and can learn to take the perspective of others, which improves decision-making. In assemblies, a similar mechanism operates. While discussing issues of mutual importance, perspective-taking leads to decision-making based on more than pre-existing interests. Through deliberation, different members of the assembly learn about others and themselves, and this influences decision-making.

Multispecies knowledge already exists, for example, at sanctuaries and in certain Indigenous communities that do not see humans as outside of nature. But the knowledge that comes from this type of engagement is in large part new, because most humans are not used to consulting other animals and plants or even listening to them at all. Politically, most human societies neglect nonhuman wisdom and ways of life.

Nonhuman animals are not used to being listened to or taken seriously in other ways. Changing human attitudes may change how nonhumans understand their position in the multispecies community and the roles they can take on. This, in turn, may influence the functioning of assemblies. Therefore, the creation of new multispecies knowledge should be taken seriously in assemblies and multispecies communities more generally.

Language and Communication[48]

While human language plays a central role in deliberation among humans, it will not be the sole or even primary tool for engaging with others in multispecies assemblies. Depending on who is involved, embodied and material expressions may play a role. Conversations may, for example, include touch, movement, observation, play, or silence. Participants will learn about the species-specific languages of others and will develop new, shared, multispecies language-games. For adult humans, listening will often be more important than speaking. Perhaps every assembly meeting should begin with human silence. As I discussed above, there is already much knowledge about deliberation with animals that can inform trajectories of multispecies deliberation. Currently, deliberation with plants and trees is underdeveloped, but there are examples of artists and thinkers who take vegetal agency seriously, such as biologist Robin Wall Kimmerer or artist and writer Miek Zwamborn.[49] These experiments can inform direct engagement with and representation of these nonhumans.

Listening

An essential task for humans in multispecies assemblies is developing new listening skills and practices.[50] Political listening in multispecies communities involves more than sitting still and using one's ears; it can also mean learning how to become acquainted with plants and trees by watching them, learning the movements of other beings through daily walks in nature or urban areas, creating spaces for others to speak and learning how to invite them in, and being open to the invitations of others. Listening is vital for understanding other beings, building new relations, and establishing consent. We currently know little about how other animals or nonhuman beings can give consent, and we must learn more about this to be able to set up respectful relations.

Meetings

In human assemblies, all who participate in the assembly come together at a given time for deliberation. This is a human preference and not suitable for many nonhuman agents, because of how they express themselves and want to relate to humans. Being present at meetings in assemblies also can be complicated because we are all so different. Some beings are diurnal (awake during the day) while others are nocturnal (awake during the night); some live in the water and others on (or in) the earth or in the sky; some sit still for much of the time, while others are continually on the move. In multispecies assemblies, actual meetings can be part of the decision-making process. Still, they will need to be supplemented by other deliberation processes, such as interventions in the land, rituals, habits, play, and other forms of political experimentation. When decisions must be made quickly for safety reasons, humans could be forced to take the lead and meet in the human way, but this would be an exception.

Movement and Process

In contrast to human assemblies and human politics more generally, in which meetings often aim for and end with a clear decision, multispecies assemblies will typically be characterized by a focus on the process of decision-making, which includes knowledge creation. While political decisions can and sometimes should be made, the aim is not to decide quickly but rather to have a good process, one that is fair and leads to greater equality. One of the things that humans can learn from nonhumans and nature is that everything is constantly changing. This affects relations, including political relations, which are not fixed but fluid and open.

Respect

While assemblies might involve differences of opinion or even conflicts, it is necessary to treat all beings in the assembly with respect. Human participants will need to be mindful and proactive about this. Most humans currently live in societies characterized by large-scale exploitation of nonhuman animals and the natural world. Many humans are so accustomed to anthropocentric domination that they do not even notice it. They perceive human supremacy as natural or necessary and the status quo as neutral.

Respect for animals first of all means not killing, capturing, or torturing them. Human participants in multispecies assemblies must also actively challenge human supremacy in discourses and practices. Under current circumstances, humans limit the freedom and agency of most other animals through land occupation, violence, processes of domestication, and in other ways. When setting up assemblies, it is important not to repeat these forms of violence, especially in the transition from an anthropocentric society to a multispecies society.

Concerning plants, respect means taking them seriously as beings, as Robin Wall Kimmerer describes in *Braiding Sweetgrass*. An attitude of respect can be expressed in different practices, such as not taking more than the plant can give when plucking parts for eating or other purposes and thanking the plant. Thanking a plant is not an act of communication with them, but it shows other humans (and perhaps other animals) that you respect the plant. For this reason, thanking can also be part of showing respect for environmental entities, for example, in rituals and ceremonies that can make up part of assembly meetings.

Developing an attitude of respect is an important ingredient of working toward multispecies assemblies and multispecies justice. While this may come easily to some individuals, societies will take time to shift. But it is also something that we can begin doing now.

Rituals and Habits

Rituals and ceremonies can have several functions in multispecies assemblies. They can express respect, for example, when humans thank plants or the land when they harvest. Rituals can also function as a tool for multispecies community—building, for example. Seasonal festivals or eating ceremonies can help us understand one another and create solidarity in multispecies communities that can inform or be part of assemblies. Greeting rituals can help set boundaries between communities and can be part of assembly meetings, too. In addition to rituals and ceremonies that have a formal function, new shared habits based on or informed by the agency of nonhumans should be part of developing stronger multispecies communities. These might also play a role in assemblies: Coming together regularly in a specific spot and showing others if you are content or not can help beings in an assembly get to know one another.

Scale

Both spatially and temporally, many beings experience life on a different scale than humans. Trees, who often have long lives and are rooted in one place, exist differently from the worms in the soil beneath them or the migrating birds who seek out shelter on their branches. The human scale is only one among many. However, issues of shared importance might cut across these dimensions and collect beings into a group, or public. A tree, worm, migrating bird, and human might exist very differently, but all will be affected by the pollution of the soil. All would benefit from a remedy. Still, this might mean that in deliberating about a common problem, varied questions and interests are at stake. Therefore, the question of scale matters in assemblies.

Scope

The scope of politics changes in multispecies assemblies. By this, I mean that some questions that may not seem political in the human case—for example, who sits where at the dinner table or who takes the initiative to play or seek out companionship—may be important topics of debate in multispecies communities. We need to rearrange our societies from the ground up, and ideas about the good life are different for different beings.

Feminists have challenged distinctions between the public and private spheres and shown that many topics seen as private by neoliberal societies—such as care and housework—are political. The private is also political in multispecies relations. Reforming societies requires attention to matters of daily life in addition to more formal political questions. Awareness that different social groups have their own scope of politics is also needed.

Place

Multispecies assemblies should be rooted in a specific place, which can be small, like the garden behind my house, but also large, like a forest or a sea. Deliberation and decision-making should ideally take place in this space. However, questions to be discussed are not limited to the space: They might stretch out globally, requiring representation of beings elsewhere.

Time

In general, multispecies assemblies will take more time and need more attention to be set up than human assemblies, especially in the beginning. As I mentioned before, in multispecies deliberation, the process might matter more than the outcome. Taking time to deliberate (including finding out how to best deliberate) matters for answering common questions and also allows for new questions to arise. Learning to see others for who they are takes time. Humans generally have less knowledge about nonhumans than fellow humans, and this kind of active, peaceful, democratic engagement across species borders is new. Nonhuman animals will also need to learn to participate in the assemblies and deal with the changed attitudes of the humans in the assembly. Because assemblies are embedded in a specific place, changes might occur during deliberation and negotiation, such as changing weather or seasons, or visits from migrating animals.

In addition to these practical considerations, time also matters from an ontological perspective. Different beings have their own temporal scales. The ex-laboratory mice I was fortunate to get to know and live with typically only live to be two years old, and during this time they pass through the whole cycle of life. Certain trees can live to be hundreds or thousands of years old, which affects how they are rooted in time and space, and they go through seasonal changes in ways very different from humans. Living slower or faster also influences if and how we can understand others. For example, many birds communicate much more rapidly than humans can detect without the aid of recordings that can be played back more slowly.

Attention to time is also necessary to connect the present to the past and the future. In multispecies assemblies, future generations should be represented, and current obligations on behalf of humans might derive from past harms. Sometimes these are clearly present in the land, as in the case of pollution, while other times they can be more symbolic.

All of these elements of time in the context of assemblies ask us to view time not only linearly but also cyclically.

A Possible Five-Step Procedure

Step 1: Setting Up the Assembly

An individual or group signals a question for an assembly, either because it concerns them or because they notice that it concerns others. This individual or group takes the initiative to convene a group of facilitators to oversee the assembly. This group of facilitators can consist of humans (including human youth), nonhuman animals, and perhaps others, as I will discuss in more detail in the next chapter. Once an assembly is established as an ongoing form of government in a given space, there will be no further need for a separate group of facilitators. (This step is only necessary for new assemblies.)

Step 2: The Scope of the Assembly

The group of facilitators maps the situation. They investigate who is affected and who should be part of the assembly, what is precisely at stake, how this can be discussed and where, who can speak for themselves versus who should be represented, and similar kinds of questions. This might already involve multispecies interaction, which I discuss in more detail when I turn to the role of animals in assemblies.

Step 3: Deliberation

The assembly comes together in person or in a mixed format including representation. The assembly deliberates using different processes of question and response. These processes can include human language, embodied non-linguistic deliberation, material and spatial processes, and other forms of communication. Decisions need to be tried out and worked through. Especially in the beginning, there will be a need for experimentation. Over time, as new habits have evolved and agents get to know each other better, discussions will become easier.

Step 4: Decision-Making

After a process of deliberation, the assembly reaches a decision. Sometimes, clear choices can be made through consensus. More often, there will be moments of decision-making that affect the course of the process but do not lead to a fixed outcome.

Step 5: Ending the Assembly

After some time, it becomes clear if the assembly is finished—choices are made—or if there is a need for an ongoing group of facilitators and/or assembly. Once an assembly is done, there is always the possibility of new information coming into view. For example, new insights can arise on behalf of one of the participating groups or new actors can arrive in a community, such as refugees of different species or migrating animals. Perhaps seasonal assemblies will need to be formed in some spaces, or assemblies that temporarily connect communities that generally avoid one another. Over time, a structure will fall into place based on the eco-cultural development of the multispecies community.

3

THE POSITION OF ANIMALS, PLANTS, HUMAN YOUTH, ENVIRONMENTAL ENTITIES, AND OTHERS IN MULTISPECIES ASSEMBLIES

Multispecies Assemblies and Animals

In short: Some animals can speak for themselves in assemblies, while others need to be represented by other animals or humans. New cultural and political habits and rituals can strengthen and improve multispecies decision-making.

Within Western democracies, nonhuman animals are not recognized as speaking beings, much less capable of political participation. At the same time, more and more research shows that many species have complex languages. For example, prairie dogs describe humans who enter their territory in detail, mentioning the color of their hair, clothing, and objects they might carry, like guns. Their language also has a grammar, and prairie dogs invent new combinations of words to describe unknown phenomena. Prairie dogs are not unique in their language use, even though how well their language has been studied by biologist Con Slobodchikoff[51] is unique. Nonhuman animals use sound, touch, scent, movements, color, gestures, and many other forms of expression to communicate with members of their own and other species. While we do not know the full extent of animal languages, we have learned that there is more to their inner and social lives than many humans think. Dolphins,[52] parrots[53] and bats, for example, have names – and bats are known to gossip.[54] We find grammatical structures, including recursion, in the songs of different species of birds.[55] The skin patterns of Caribbean reef squid can be seen as a language in color.[56]

Languages—or, perhaps better, language-games—are not just species-specific: Humans have a long-shared history with many nonhuman animal species, which influenced the capacities of beings of different species for understanding one another. Horses can use symbols to communicate their preferences,[57] or just move humans in the right direction by using head movements. Domesticated cats teach themselves to meow to attract human attention.[58] Dogs and humans have co-evolved, and both species have influenced the characteristics of the other—some biologists even think that humans may have started to use language in relation to dogs.[59] Humans can correctly interpret dog moods when they hear them bark or growl on tape or see their facial expressions; dogs can also read human sounds and faces.[60] When dogs and humans who are friends gaze into each other's eyes, they create oxytocin, the 'cuddle hormone,' something which also happens between lovers and between parents and their babies.[61] There is no clear line between human language and the languages of other animals: There are parallels, resemblances, and differences between languages of different species.

For assemblies, species-specific languages are important—it helps to know what someone says when they speak to you in their language. But even more importantly, especially in the context of developing multispecies assemblies, is the fact that there are many shared language-games between humans and other animals. Some of these are extensive and involve much interaction, for example between working animals and humans, or companion animals and humans. Many companion animals are bilingual and also speak some human. Other already-existing multispecies language-games are more casual, such as greeting practices, or only occur once, such as acts of assistance (like dolphins who rescue humans). Yet other multispecies language-games involve violence or conflict. For example, animals who are hunted by humans change their lifestyle and approach toward humans and teach their children to avoid humans.

In addition to these common language-games, humans should also recognize that human language has been shaped by the presence and agency of other animals, as philosopher Raimond Gaita has suggested.[62] Our understanding of a concept such as 'love' or 'friendship' is co-shaped by the forms of love and friendship that we see in other animals and the love and friendship we might share with them.

For multispecies assemblies, this means that there is already quite an extensive repertoire of understanding that makes direct collective decision-making possible between humans and many other animals—domesticated, wild, or liminal. Some animals who do not want to be part of assemblies can be represented by other animals. For example, shy street dogs might be represented by outgoing members of their community in deliberation about a shared space. Others will need to be represented by humans, including animals who are very different from humans in terms of perception and experience or about whom humans currently do not know much. In assemblies, we should develop better forms of direct interaction *and* better forms of representation informed by animal agency. Because of human bias in science and philosophy, there is not much research about procedures through which humans can represent more-than-human beings respectfully and truthfully.[63] Similar to further developing systems of multispecies political participation, developing systems of nonhuman representation requires careful attention and the creation of new knowledge.

Including Animals in Assemblies

Step 1: Setting up the Assembly

Humans can initiate an assembly that includes animals because they notice the need for it, but other animals can do so, too. They can signal a problem or political question, individually or as part of a group with others of their own or other species. Animals also can be active members of permanent assemblies and initiate embodied deliberation as well as material and spatial forms of interaction.

Step 2: The Scope of the Assembly

Determining who is affected by the question to be discussed in the assembly and who should be consulted is primarily a human task. Still, other animals can assist and point humans in specific directions. For example, they can show whether or not they want to be part of the deliberation and direct attention to what they want to discuss.

Step 3: Deliberation

Many animals can participate in embodied, spatial, and material deliberation processes. Domesticated animals and humans share a sizeable cultural repertoire of interaction that can be drawn upon. Others, such as liminal and wild animals like songbirds or bees, also already have many ways of understanding the humans with whom they share habitats and vice versa. The questions to be discussed and the people involved in the assembly determine the methods needed. In processes of deliberation, species is not the only factor that counts. Social relations do too, as well as individual characters and preferences. Just as humans have different personalities, some animals will be more curious about finding new solutions, others will be more conservative, and others might not be interested in doing politics at all.

Step 4: Decision-Making

In some cases, there will be a clear decision, such as when a group of animals decides to leave a certain area or a community finds an equitable balance for living in the same habitat and sharing resources. In other cases, there might be more to discuss, or new information that arises in the process. Processes of multispecies deliberation can include multiple moments of decision-making.

Step 5: Ending the Assembly

When a decision is made by the collective or even a group of animals, as in the case of leaving the shared habitat, assemblies can end. In other cases, there will be a need for ongoing deliberation. When assemblies end, there is always the possibility of new information that calls for revising earlier decisions or judgments. The different beings involved in the assembly bring their expertise into the multispecies community and new assemblies. There is a close connection between assemblies and multispecies community building. Equality among assembly members will improve when the multispecies community becomes more solid. Living differently will lead to new forms of multispecies knowledge and politics. This also works the other way around: Assemblies can improve the multispecies community.

Multispecies Assemblies and Plants

In short: Plants need to be represented by humans, but decisions should be made in their presence as much as possible, and if new forms of democratic interaction turn out to be possible, this could change. Representation should be informed by engagement with the plants in question and knowledge about them. Rituals of respect (like thanking and greeting) should be part of honoring relations in multispecies communities. Attending to plants and strengthening relations of care (through collective practices) can teach humans to be more attuned to their needs and strengthen their position in assemblies.

The political relations humans in western parts of the world have with plants resemble those with nonhuman animals in important ways. Like animals, plants are considered voiceless and are not taken seriously in political systems. Their ways of being are generally contrasted with those of humans in binary opposition, leading to knowledge structures that obscure plant being and deny their agency. Recent studies in biology show that plants, like animals, have complex systems of communication, actively shape social relations with members of their own and other species, and have the capacity to experience and respond to stress.[64] Furthermore, there are no clear lines between animals and plants, and both are heterogeneous groups—oak trees have little in common with algae, and pigs are very different from butterflies. These differences matter concerning social relations, political voice, and many other elements relevant to deliberation and decision-making. But there is no prima facie reason to exclude plants from deliberative systems beforehand.

The lives of humans and plants are entangled in many ways. Ecofeminists, critical plant studies scholars, and other critical thinkers have emphasized the importance of recognizing these entanglements and stressed the need for a relational approach to studying plants and improving relat ions.[65] Concepts such as kinship and interdependence can play an important role in this process. As I mentioned before, this way of thinking about human-plant relations is not new. Many Indigenous traditions use different epistemological and cosmological frameworks for thinking about plants and recognize plants as fellow creatures, communities, and/or teachers. Robin Wall Kimmerer describes ideas and practices that express this view of co-being, for example regarding eating plants and keeping ecosystems healthy.[66] In multispecies assemblies, plants do not need to develop new capacities. Instead, humans need to learn to see them differently.

In thinking about plants and assemblies, or politics more generally, this gestalt shift includes not just recognizing plant ways of perceiving and shaping the world; it also calls for recognition that we *already* form collectives with plants in different ways. The human focus on species is often unhelpful and leads to what I earlier described as *species skepticism*. While species-specific attributes matter, all living beings are part of networks in which other beings exercise agency and affect each other. There are many similarities and differences among actors, as well as many forms of understanding and misunderstanding. Viewing the world as alive, and others as agentive beings, is necessary for overcoming human exceptionalism in politics. Similar to improving interactions with nonhuman animals, improved relationships with plants will require multispecies education, new forms of representation, and new forms of direct communication.

Including Plants in Assemblies

Step 1: Setting up the Assembly

Plants cannot take the initiative for an assembly, but their behavior can show that something is not going well in a given environment. Humans and other animals—for example grazing animals or sea mammals—can pick up on that and take the initiative for an assembly. In ongoing assemblies, plants can take part in material deliberative practices, but political experimentation is needed to find out how.

Step 2: The Scope of the Assembly

Plants will often be part of assemblies, either because they are part of the same assemblages as humans and other animals, or because their interests are at stake.

Step 3: Deliberation

Embodied, material, and spatial discussions with plants can take two routes. In some instances, humans can actively address plants by changing the soil, the landscape, planting practices, or otherwise. Plants can contribute to decision-making processes in ongoing assemblies with their agency. They might also be part of forests or other communities that influence other beings directly as a collective. More often, a model of representation and translation will be required, especially given the current domination of humans and the general lack of knowledge about plants. By a model of representation and translation, I mean that certain humans take it upon themselves to articulate the position of plants and their interests with regard to flourishing to others in the assembly. This can be done in human language, but also through guarding the land and sending a message to others (like nonhuman animals) in that way. Translation can be done by botanists, plant biologists, ecologists, activists, farmers, or others who have specific local knowledge about or experience with plants. Deliberation about plants should take place in the presence of those whom it concerns, and be informed by their presence. Humans should recognize that plants provide others in the assembly with food and oxygen.

Step 4: Decision-Making

Decision-making with and about plants will be similar to decision-making processes with animals. Sometimes there will be a clear end to a discussion because a problem has been solved, and sometimes negotiations and interactions will be ongoing. Decision-making with plants also differs from decision-making with animals, because human representation of plants relies more heavily on human modes of decision-making. Political engagement with plants also asks for more imagination, for example in setting up experiments for deliberation and decision-making, than deliberation and decision-making with animals.

Step 5: Ending the Assembly

After a period of embodied human-vegetal deliberation, there could be a final outcome, or balance in the land, but it could also be that new information continues to bring new challenges, or that new knowledge about plants changes the situation.

Environmental Entities

In short: Environmental entities must be represented by humans or other animals in assemblies, but decisions should ideally be taken in their presence. Rituals of respect (like thanking and greeting) can be part of honoring relations with environmental entities. Spending time with them instead of seeing them solely as background to the actions of animals and plants can improve human judgment.

Environmental entities like rivers, seas, mountains, forests, and gardens provide a holding environment for multispecies communities. They are the places in which beings interact and speak about questions of common importance. They can also be communities themselves, for example in the case of a forest. Because I already discussed animals and plants, I will leave the question of the environmental entity as a community of living beings (for example, a forest) aside, and here focus on environmental entities who are not considered beings in the Western tradition, such as mountains, seas, and rivers. Relations between humans and environmental entities are different from relations with animals or plants. Environmental entities exercise agency in a different way and have different interests. How to compare these is something that should be discussed in assemblies, and in these, environmental entities should be represented by humans who are suitably knowledgeable and imaginative to do so adequately.

Western attitudes toward the agency of environmental entities are currently ambiguous. While they are not viewed as beings, their agency is often recognized by humans. For example, the force of the North Sea in the Netherlands is well understood by beings living in coastal areas in the Netherlands, even though this sea is not represented politically or taken seriously as an agent or being in any official way. Regarding and representing environmental entities as beings, instead of taking them for granted as objects or as a mute background to action can help humans learn to live better on the planet and is part of a respectful attitude toward nonhumans in assemblies.

Including Environmental Entities

Step 1: Setting Up the Assembly

Environmental entities can signal a problem in ways that others can detect—a sea can change color due to pollution, glaciers can melt, and forests can lose foliage. Humans or other animals can notice this and take the initiative for an assembly. Environmental entities cannot be part of the group of facilitators, who must therefore take great care to ensure that their interests are represented at every stage.

Step 2: The Scope of the Assembly

In mapping who is affected by a given problem and who should be part of the assembly, humans should always consider the space in which the assembly is rooted. They should pay attention to this holding environment and the different relations beings have to it, which matters for determining who should be included in assemblies. For example, if there is pollution in the North Sea, the animals and plants who live in it should be part of the multispecies assembly that discusses how to deal with it. The sea itself should also be part of the assembly through representation because focusing on the sea as a whole allows humans to assess the whole network of relations.

Step 3 and 4: Deliberation and Decision-Making

In the process of deliberation and decision-making, environmental entities should be represented by humans, and treated with respect by the beings who take part in the assembly. Ideally, deliberation takes place in the presence of the entity involved.

Step 5: Ending the assembly

Ongoing ecological processes, such as those in forests, rivers, and seas, will co-determine if assemblies end or are ongoing. In permanent assemblies, environmental entities should be continually represented.

Multispecies Assemblies and Human Youth

In short: Like animals, youth can sometimes speak for themselves and sometimes need to be represented. New cultural and political practices, for example, based on play or multispecies education, can strengthen and improve youth's political participation, thereby improving multispecies decision-making.

Political participation and representation of youth (of all species, but here I will focus on human youth specifically) matter because youth have their own perspectives on life that might deviate from the perspectives of adults. They too should have the right to co-create the conditions under which they live. In the context of the ecological crises that characterize the Anthropocene, youth's political participation becomes even more pressing because political decisions made now impact their futures.

Similar to animals, human youth were long seen as incapable of political decision-making, and it was presumed that political participation did not interest them. This is currently being challenged from different angles. In academia, there is much literature about youth's political participation and rights, in which scholars like John Wall argue that youth have a political voice and should have the right to express that and be heard.[67] In political practice, we find institutions aimed at giving youth a voice, such as youth parliaments and city councils. Because adult decision-makers do not always listen to the youth participating in such initiatives, there are questions regarding their influence on adult politics. Still, these institutions show that it is possible for youth to participate in democracy and express themselves politically.

Many youth themselves challenge their exclusion from decision-making, for example, through climate protests.[68] While the voices of youth are currently underrepresented in climate assemblies, many young people are already active in climate resistance. Young people also may organize themselves in opposition to the state by initiating and taking part in practices that challenge existing hierarchies, for example, by claiming public spaces like squares and parks.[69]

Like animals and plants, youth are a heterogeneous group. Their role in assemblies might sometimes be very similar to that of adults, in the case of older youth, or quite different when children are very young. While interaction can be language-based, youth can also bring new political styles and practices into the assembly, such as drawing, play, or storytelling. Importantly, like animals and plants, youth can be teachers because they have their own perspective on life. Life is new for them. Furthermore, research shows that younger children are not yet socialized into anthropocentrism, which gives them another perspective on questions of common concern and multispecies relations.[70]

Including Youth in Assemblies

Step 1: Setting up the Assembly

The assembly can be initiated by youth, by youth and adults working together, or by youth as part of a multispecies group. Youth of different ages and backgrounds can take part in the organizing group of facilitators and bring their own ideas and perspectives into the discussion. Youth pay attention to other details than adult humans, which is important in setting up assemblies and finding out who should be involved.

Step 2: The Scope of the Assembly

Finding out what should be discussed and who can participate or should be represented works roughly the same as with animals. Including youth in assemblies also shows the importance of attending to the temporal dimensions of deliberation: While animals, plants, and humans all benefit from sustainable relations, the time scale to be considered is different for oaks, human youth and elderly humans, mice, bees, and dogs. Finding out who is affected is, therefore, not only a spatial endeavor but also requires identifying who will be affected in the future, as far as possible.

Step 3: Deliberation

Speaking with youth can involve human words, human or multispecies embodied communication, play, art, and other forms of deliberation. Youth may develop new ways of deliberating with nonhuman animals and plants because young people take them more seriously than adult humans tend to do.

Step 4: Decision-Making

In decision-making processes, the role of youth is similar to that of adult humans and animals.

Step 5: Ending the Assembly

Youth can be part of a longstanding political system, as is already the case in the Rebel Zapatista Autonomous Municipalities, in which all youth aged 12 and above can participate in government. They can also be part of temporal assemblies. When youth are part of assemblies, the culture of a community changes because they learn to interact with others differently from a young age.

Multispecies Assemblies and Other Others

Thus far, I have focused on the participation of living non-human beings, human youth, and environmental entities in assemblies and sketched how this can look. This required drawing rough lines, such as those between humans and animals or animals and plants. In reality, the borders between these categories are porous. I also did not discuss fungi and bacteria. Bacteria affect other beings and societies. Scientists find out more about fungi every day, including their ways of communicating with other entities like trees.[71] So, it could very well be that they would need to be represented in assemblies, either as single entities or as parts of more extensive networks. My ideas about plants and natural entities can guide thinking about these nonhumans in assemblies, but their precise position in assemblies needs more reflection and experimentation.

All beings participating in assemblies are part of networks stretching out in space and time. Those existing now are connected to those who came before and those who will come into being in the future. In assemblies, future generations should be represented by adult humans, youth, and/or nonhuman animals if their interests are at stake, which will often be the case. Ancestors should be considered to develop a fair system of reparations and also symbolically, in the case of extinct plants and animals and groups of humans from which there were no survivors. It is important to recognize that there are not only human ancestors and future generations but also animal and plant ancestors and future generations. Even when nonhuman animals (seemingly) do not care about their ancestors, it might be important to honor them or acknowledge earlier violence from humans, for example, through ceremonies or rituals. How and by whom future generations should be represented precisely depends on the questions at stake, and this is something that should be decided by the assembly.

Lastly, including environmental entities in assemblies raises the question of including things. David Schlosberg and Christine Winter write that the border between living and non-living matter is problematic when we want to rethink justice and that those working toward justice should also consider things.[72] The category 'things' contains many different objects. Schlosberg and Winter discuss consumer items, the use function of which is most important. They argue that nonliving matter matters because it stands for invisible processes that might involve labor or extraction that influence the lives of many. This is convincing, but views things only instrumentally. For assemblies, that would mean that nonliving matter does not need to get a seat at the table but should be a topic of discussion. There are also other kinds of things that have aesthetic or democratic value. Art objects have aesthetic value for societies and can generate meaning in human communities and multispecies relations. Furthermore, things can and should play a role in deliberation and decision-making because they offer a way of engaging with others without using human language. For example, games and toys can facilitate conversations with youth or animals. Things can thus play different roles in assemblies that need to be developed further through multispecies interaction.

Finally, there are also unknown beings that might be affected by decisions made by an assembly. These can include beings who live further away, hide, or about whom we are unaware. These beings can be represented if we know they are there but cannot establish direct interaction. Sometimes, they cannot because they fall outside of the scope of our understanding and knowledge. I mentioned before that assemblies should be open-ended. Knowing that there can always be unknown others should be an invitation to be curious about what surrounds us and careful in what we do.

4

TWO EXAMPLES OF MULTISPECIES ASSEMBLIES

Example 1: The Future of a Tree

A storm damages a large willow tree in a courtyard garden between three blocks of houses. The tree can be saved by constructing a support apparatus for its heavy lower branches on one side. Still, some of the humans living in houses around the courtyard garden want it taken down because the downed tree means that they get more natural light in their homes and also because it is less costly than rescuing it. They prefer the light not only for personal reasons but also for the sake of the community: The tree's shade makes it difficult to grow vegetables in part of the garden. Other humans are attached to the tree, enjoy the shade that it provides on warm days, or have other reasons why they want to care for it. In the tree lives a woodpecker, and while there are more trees around in which the woodpecker could live, they clearly prefer this tree. City pigeons also like to sit in this tree during the day, and two wood pigeons sleep on one of its branches at night. Some children who live in the houses surrounding the garden like to climb in the tree. They made a ladder up to one of the low branches and like to sit there. One of their companion cats usually joins them. Other animals also use the tree for shelter or enjoy its shade. Some insects live in the grooves of its bark.

Step 1: Setting up the Assembly

Humans take the initiative for the assembly, and the tree itself strongly influences those who do—one of them, for example, grew up in one of the houses overlooking the courtyard and has fond memories of this tree. Another human taking the initiative has strong relations with the birds, for whom the tree is an integral part of daily life, or even their home, in the case of the woodpecker and the two wood pigeons who sleep on one of the branches.

Step 2: The Scope of the Assembly

The facilitators investigate who should be consulted: human neighbors, including children, bird residents and migrating birds who use the tree, and companion animals. The tree itself, as well as the other trees in the garden and the insects who live there, should be represented.

Step 3: Deliberation

The human members of the assembly meet outside in front of the tree several times and deliberate about their standpoints. Some designated humans speak for the trees and the insects. They either have experience with these beings and/or have learned about them, which includes spending time with them. At the same time, spatial experiments are set up to ask the birds and insects whether they want to move to the other trees. Because the humans have little experience with multispecies deliberation, they draw on interactions that already exist, primarily about food and safe places to rest and nest. They set out to make other spaces in the garden more attractive for the birds by leaving the berries they usually pick on the elder and the currant bush and sprinkling seeds and grains for them. They also hang a woodpecker box on one of the remaining trees. For the insects, they plant flowering plants in other parts of the garden. Someone comes up with the idea to make part of the garden that is not used anyway a no-entry zone for humans so that the other animals feel more at ease there.

Step 4: Decision-Making

None of the birds like the other trees. They eat the berries, but they continue to use the old tree as they did before. The insects remain where they are. The no-entry zone becomes popular among songbirds, who also begin to visit the fallen tree. The human children favor keeping the tree because now it looks even more like a castle. Someone brings in the idea of gardening on the roofs of the buildings, which the others like. Slowly, the humans who had preferred the tree to be allowed to die come to see the value of the tree for the rest of the community. They learn that because the top branches need to be taken down, there will be more light anyway, at least for some time. The decision is made to support the tree and keep it.

Step 5: Ending the Assembly

The following spring, the woodpecker leaves to take up residence in the nearby park. But the community appreciates the tree more than before and better understands its social and ecological function, so there is no need for a new assembly. Those who took part in the assembly have developed skills that they can use in other assemblies and the wider community, and the communication between the city pigeons and the humans has improved. The humans are also more attuned to the trees and other plants in the garden, and continue to explore how to communicate with the ants and other insects who live there.

Example 2: Transitioning to a Multispecies Community

In the Netherlands, intensive animal agriculture needs to be reformed because of the 'nitrogen crisis,' an ecological and political crisis caused by human impact on the nitrogen cycle. In short, the soil around farms and in nature reserves is polluted by reactive nitrogen compounds, primarily ammonia and nitrogen oxides. This is caused mainly by animal farming, mostly dairy farming. Dutch Natura 2000 nature reserves fall under European legislation aimed at protecting biodiversity, so the Dutch government was required to take measures to reduce nitrogen pollution.[73] They first lowered the speed limit in the whole country, but this was not effective enough. This prompted them to set limits for emissions on farms. Stricter regulation led to farmers' protests and a new farmers' political party (the BoerBurgerBeweging, which translates as the FarmerCitizenMovement). The government now buys out farmers to reduce livestock emissions. This is currently voluntary but might be mandatory in the future.[74]

While the pollution has awakened strong forces to protect the current interests of farmers, we could also imagine that this crisis could be the start of a more just way of sharing the land with nonhuman others, which would require speaking with these others to ask them how they view the future. For epistemic reasons and reasons of justice, a multispecies assembly should decide upon questions about the future of the land and of developing more just and caring multispecies ways of living.

Let us imagine an assembly that would focus on five farms near a nature reserve that want to transition to multispecies justice. The space in and about which they deliberate encompasses the farms, the meadows between the farms, and the nature reserve, where only one type of grass currently grows. The nature reserve should also be part of the assembly because some of the animals living there used to live on the land that farmers now occupy, and the forest was cut down by humans, too.

Not all humans feel up to this transition. Some farmers leave. The ones who stay change to veganic farming. Two new humans arrive who want to set up an anti-capitalist vegan farm on one of the farms, and two other new humans wish to set up an ecological art space at another farm. The remaining buildings are used as housing or spaces for ethical experimentation—for example, to find out how the more-than-human animals can contribute to the design and decoration of the space—but some of the barns need to be demolished to free up space. Some animals associate these barns with violence and do not want to go near them.

The humans on the farms are part of the assembly, and some have children who will also be part of the assembly. A few humans from the nearby town also participate in the assembly. More importantly than the humans, there are the cows who had been used in dairy farming, some of them pregnant, two horses, four dogs, four barn cats and two house cats, ten chickens (not used in intensive agriculture, but raised as backyard chickens). Communities of liminal mice and wild mice live in the area, as do meadow birds and songbirds, insects, frogs, fishes, hares, and rabbits. There are also the animals who live in the nearby nature reserve and migrating animals who visit it annually. Different plants grow in the area. There is the grass and some wildflowers on the fields. In and around the nature reserve grow native plants and trees, such as black alders, oaks, silver poplars, and willows. There are also several environmental entities, such as the fields, the small rivers and canals that separate them, the forest, and the swamp in the nature reserve.

Step 1: Setting up the Assembly

The humans who initiate the transition to a multispecies community set up the assembly and ensure that everyone who lives in the area can speak or is represented while also mapping who lives in the surrounding areas. Moving from a human-dominated model to a multispecies model gives humans this responsibility, and humans have a specific responsibility in this particular transition, given the extreme human violence that shaped the place in the past decades. Two of the older youth are part of the group of facilitators.

Step 2: The scope of the Assembly

The facilitators look for who should be part of the assembly, who can speak for themselves, who should be represented and in which way, and how they can set up long trajectories of deliberation. Humans and many of the other animals involved, like the chickens and the cows, can speak for themselves, while certain other actors, like the forest or the fishes, will need to be represented.

Step 3: Deliberation

The community begins to deliberate. The main topic of the conversation at this stage is how to move from a human-centered society to a multispecies community. This includes asking the domesticated animals if they want to be part of a multispecies community with humans and establishing an understanding with the other communities in the area, like those of the crows and the liminal mice. They discuss who lives where, how to fairly share the land, and how to shape relations between and within communities. To answer these questions, they need time, multispecies education, and learning. For example, the cows need time to get used to different relations with humans and choose if they want to stay around, build or rebuild their own community, and further develop their own culture. The soil needs time to recover from decades of pesticides; plants need time to regrow; and insects who used to live in the area in earlier times might return.

To facilitate multispecies learning, processes of embodied and material deliberation are set up between different agents. The cows, chickens, dogs, and cats let humans know where they want to live. The humans begin to plant crops for food, a spatial intervention that will solicit responses by animals, such as birds and insects, and lead to new vegetation. The human artists develop experiments to get to know one another better in collaboration with beings of different species. All of the humans involved meet regularly in different spaces, on the fields, in the forest, and near the swamp to get to know these environmental entities and their inhabitants. The assembly also develops new forms of multispecies meetings based on play and habits – here, the youth and companion animals take the lead. Through living together differently, new rituals of greeting and thanking come into being. The human artists work on further developing these in collaboration with the more-than-humans who are interested.

Steps 4 & 5: Decision-Making and Ending the Assembly

To establish a community, multiple decisions will need to be made. Some will be more or less final. For example, the cows will settle in their preferred space and develop new habits. The anti-capitalist vegan farm adopted a model of farming in which fifty percent of the land is for nonhumans, ten percent for humans, and the rest is shared.[75] After some initial difficulties and misunderstandings, all inhabitants of the area now have a routine. The artistic humans have transformed one of the barns into a meeting space for social art projects and communal knowledge creation. The children have set up a multispecies playground, and the chickens, dogs and cats helped in developing the playground equipment. There are common rules and habits with regard to the plants, the forests, and the water, but humans are still learning to reposition themselves and better see others. There are new rituals and ceremonies to express this attitude.

Much of the deliberation is ongoing: between residents, between residents and visitors, and between environmental entities and the animal (including human) residents—especially as the forest is now gaining territory. Developing multispecies education is also an ongoing process in which humans and nonhumans take part, and the same is true for creating new structures of care. The group of facilitators that organizes the assembly meetings is no longer necessary because there are norms and habits in place and a flexible system of multispecies meetings and deliberation. However, this could change when new circumstances give rise to new and more specific questions for the assembly. The aim at this stage is to further focus on inclusion and co-government with nonhumans. How this develops depends on all agents in the community.

5

STEPS TOWARDS MULTISPECIES ASSEMBLIES

My aim in this text was not to develop a full theory of multispecies assembly. This is not possible from behind a computer, nor is it desirable because I am only a human. But I did want to show that we can begin to investigate political questions with other animals, plants, and human youth and that we should begin to do so. The model I sketched is very open and meant to provide a starting point for new multispecies political decision-making. Overall, it is more democratic than existing anthropocentric models of politics. Of course, there is room for improvement in many respects, for example with regard to the precise details of the procedure, the normative background of assemblies, and their scope. All of this will have to be further developed in collaborative practice with nonhumans. Time will have to tell if assemblies are the best possible model for doing multispecies politics. We can only find out by experimenting. I therefore want to end with a call for action. Multispecies justice seems far away, and multispecies assemblies cannot be set up by everyone, but there are many ways in which we can work toward a better society for all. As a conclusion to this text, I will mention three—political change, repositioning the human, and building stronger multispecies communities—but there are many more.

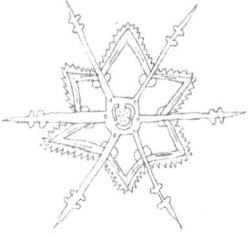

From Anthropocentric to Multispecies Politics

In Chapter 1, I discussed some examples of already existing more-than-human politics, such as the rights of nature movement and animal sanctuaries that function as multispecies communities. Humans also try to move away from anthropocentric politics in other ways, such as animal rights activism and multispecies climate activism that challenges anthropocentric politics. Academic activism aims to contribute to other ways of living with nonhuman beings by creating knowledge that does not center humans.

Political parties can also contribute to the movement toward non-anthropocentric politics. Even when animal parties are small, they can make a difference in political discourse and legislation through agenda-setting and exerting influence on other parties. The Dutch Party for the Animals is a good example of this. The Party for the Animals has been part of the Dutch government for the past twenty years, on the national, provincial, and local levels, and in the water authority. While their numeral power is still limited, they have a strong voice in public debate and motivate other parties to consider animal interests. Over time, they have moved from focusing mainly on animals to defending a holistic approach to politics, in which care is central. They are also the only party in the Netherlands to oppose economic growth. Furthermore, they offer skills and knowledge to young humans who want to be active in politics to improve the world.

These different examples can all contribute to multispecies justice. Because they emphasize the interests and agency of more-than-human beings, they can affect political and cultural structures, which can pave the way for assemblies. At the same time, setting up small experimental assemblies can inform these movements in turn. Assemblies would lead to a better understanding of the perspective of more-than-human beings and open up new ways of thinking about democracy. Moving from anthropocentric politics to multispecies politics in this way is not only important for the others with whom we share the world and for ecological reasons. It is also part of creating a democratic model that is sustainable in a time in which the limits of existing models of representative democracy are becoming increasingly clear.

Repositioning the Human

An important part of working toward ecopolitical change is decentering the human. Human exceptionalism currently guides many of the dominant narratives in society, not just about what it means to be human and what animals, plants, or nature are, but also about what a good life entails and what progress means for societies. Geographer Krithika Srinivasan draws attention to the fact that anthropocentrism has strongly influenced how we think about development and progress.[76] Western societies currently view progress narrowly, as human economic progress, but increasingly discover that this is harmful for themselves and others. According to Srinivasan, developing an alternative view of progress should go hand in hand with developing an alternative view of what it means to be human, which is based on the understanding that humans are animals too. This entails different things, like redistributing risks more equally between species and understanding that human well-being is intrinsically connected to the well-being of nonhumans. Living well with others includes friction, and embracing that will lead to new difficulties. But it also opens up the way to a more connected way of being human, beyond capitalist and consumer-based ways of being.

Reformulating what it means to be human and providing alternatives to neoliberal images of well-being may seem like a large and abstract goal, but we can all pursue it by building stronger multispecies communities, interacting differently with fellow humans, and changing cultural habits, practices, and norms.

One way of doing this is by creating new traditions or changing existing traditions so that they no longer center humans and are not violent toward others. What and how we eat has great cultural importance for many humans. Initiatives that promote vegan cooking and eating and that connect eating well to living well can contribute to eco-social change. For example, the Black Veganism movement connects questions of social justice, heritage, animal rights, and environmental concerns to eating differently and offers another way of honoring the past and its traditions while changing the future.[77] Another example concerns Eid al-Adha, the Feast of Sacrifice, which traditionally involves the sacrifice of animals. Vegan Muslim activists ask members of their community to donate money instead and eat plant-based food. Traditions can also have a more symbolic or educational function in human communities. Think, for example, of silent marches that commemorate animal victims of human violence in agriculture, labs, and elsewhere. Memorial statues for animals who were put to work in war zones are also examples of paying tribute to animals.

Stories can play a role in changing narratives around what it means to be human. Books, films, and visual art can reimagine relations and show the world differently. The growing attention to animal and vegetal agency in art and experiments in creating art together with other beings disrupt strict boundaries between humans and other beings. In this context, it is essential to understand that making multispecies art is political and takes place in a world in which nonhumans are exploited. Therefore, it is critical not to repeat stereotypes and oppression while trying to make liberatory art.

How we use language matters too. Forester Peter Wohlleben, for example, uses concepts normally reserved for human behavior to explain tree behavior.[78] While this may stretch the meaning of certain concepts, it also helps humans understand the family resemblances between how trees live together and interact and their own forms of communication and community. In a very different realm, genres of writing that rely heavily on words, like poetry and novels, can disrupt delineations between humans and others through form. One example of this is the work of writer and artist Miek Zwamborn, who writes about algae in a way that resembles their forms of being.[79] We might also need new genres of writing to express the challenges of our time. In *Summertime. Reflections on a Vanishing Future*, philosopher Danielle Celermajer shows that we need a different kind of nature writing in a world characterized by ecological collapse.[80] Celermajer writes about the bushfires in Australia from 2019 to 2020 and draws attention to their devastating impact on the different beings and communities that were affected by imagining their perspectives. This not only helps to show the true scope of the events but also offers an alternative way of being for humans, one that is attentive to the experience of others and acknowledges the multitude of connections between different beings. Finally, attending to the many ways language works between humans can also help humans become more attentive to the forms of language that other beings use.

Building Multispecies Communities

One of the most important ways we can work toward multispecies assemblies is by strengthening multispecies elements in society. This can be done in many different ways, such as through developing new forms of multispecies education, finding new ways of sharing spaces with other beings, creating new rituals (including greeting and thanking rituals), developing stronger practices of care (including health care), inventing new ways of tending to the land or returning to old ways, and developing new forms of transport that are safer for more-than-human beings. Creating a more robust multispecies infrastructure can provide a basis for multispecies political structures.

New practices of multispecies education should be developed together with more-than-human animals and human youth.[81] As I already mentioned, human children are currently socialized into anthropocentric thinking as they grow up, while research shows that younger children are not speciesist. Learning about and with nonhumans by playing together, watching others, and undertaking activities in nature can be part of an alternative to anthropocentric education. The experiences and standpoints of the youth themselves can help develop this further. Multispecies education is also important for other animals so that we can all learn to share our lives or common habitats in better ways. Of course, animals can be teachers too, regarding both the content and methods of learning. Further developing multispecies practice-based learning will allow all involved to gain new knowledge about the others with whom they learn. Multispecies learning should also be part of academic studies that create knowledge about animals, plants, and ecosystems.

Another type of activity that can be developed is multispecies rituals. With nonhuman animals, these can take the form of a party or eating together in more equal ways. We also need common grieving and remembrance rituals to help shape experiences of mourning and loss in multispecies communities. Perhaps multispecies rituals can also help animals (including humans) deal with the losses related to ecological changes following the climate crisis. Seasonal changes can be the basis for multispecies rituals and habits, too – when it gets colder, our habits change, and spring brings joy for many beings. Greeting rituals foster non-violent encounters and can have other functions for different beings. Between animals (including humans) greeting rituals can establish an intersubjective understanding between individuals or communities. Between humans and plants or environmental entities, greeting and thanking rituals can express an attitude of respect. The same is true with regard to ancestors and the dead—many humans greet the dead when they see their photograph, speak with them if they miss them or have a question, and visit their graves on their birthday or other specific dates of the year.

New practices of care need to be developed in order to provide good lives to those animals who are victims of human cruelty in agriculture and science. For example, when the laboratory mice I adopted were ill, the only treatments available were painkillers, antibiotics, or euthanasia, even though there was much knowledge about their bodies. We also need new practices of care for the land and water in the context of ongoing ecological degradation due to human acts. We currently have no answer to the extreme forest fires of the past years on different continents, the heatwaves in the seas, or the melting glaciers. While we might not be able to end them, we can change how we respond to them.

Care involves more than attending to the physical and mental health of different beings or the ecological health of environmental entities. Conceptualizing multispecies care as an alternative to the neoliberal ethos of consumerist disinterest in others can spark us to rethink relations more generally. Working toward multispecies justice in politics, activism, academia, education, or other ways involves more than changing the content of the conversation. It also calls for creating more respectful and sustainable institutions and practices beyond current use-based paradigms. Much interaction among humans, and between humans and other beings, now follows a capitalist logic based on efficiency and use. But this is not necessary. Other relations exist. I discussed many examples of these in earlier chapters, but those fortunate enough to share their lives with nonhumans can learn about other ways of living and caring from them.

In the Eyes of Others

Glimpses of another world are already visible. They are visible in human practices and in the practices and ways of being of nonhumans. It is hard to be hopeful in a world that is characterized by so much violence, but it is equally hard to remain indifferent when you are lucky enough to get to know the gentleness and values of street dogs and laboratory mice, as I have been. There is life outside human society. Many worlds exist within this world, and reaching them can be as easy as going outside and taking a walk in a forest. Or sitting in a garden.

Maybe we only really exist in the eyes of other animals. I once wrote this in a poem, and that is how I often feel. I exist in the eyes and minds of the cats and horses with whom I have shared my life, the eyes of the guinea pigs and the dogs and the mice, the eyes of the house mice and the birds in the garden, the eyes of the frogs and the toads and the salamanders. Living a good life for me is intertwined with being a good person for them.

Life manifests itself differently in and through different beings. Becoming aware of that is a source of great beauty, joy, and sorrow. But it also means that we do not have to live alone. There are others who can keep us company and show us the way. That is all, and it could be enough.

ENDNOTES

1. Nussbaum, Martha C. *Justice for animals: Our collective responsibility*. Simon and Schuster, 2023.

2. Donaldson, Sue, and Will Kymlicka. *Zoopolis: A political theory of animal rights*. Oxford University Press, 2011.

3. Adams, Carol J., and Lori Gruen. "Ecofeminist footings." *Ecofeminism: Feminist intersections with other animals and the earth* (2022): 1-43.

4. Bennett, Jane. *Influx and efflux: Writing up with Walt Whitman*. Duke University Press, 2020.

5. Lawrence, Anna M. "Listening to plants: Conversations between critical plant studies and vegetal geography." *Progress in Human Geography* 46.2 (2022): 629-651.

6. See for example: Wall Kimmerer, Robin. *Braiding sweetgrass: Indigenous wisdom, scientific knowledge and the teachings of plants*. Milkweed editions, 2013. and Simpson, Leanne Betasamosake. As we have always done: Indigenous freedom through radical resistance. U of Minnesota Press, 2017.

7. Plumwood, Val. "Nature in the active voice." *The handbook of contemporary animism*. Routledge, 2014. 441-453.

8. Wells, Rebecca, Candice Howarth, and Lina I. Brand-Correa. "Are citizen juries and assemblies on climate change driving democratic climate policymaking? An exploration of two case studies in the UK." *Climatic Change* 168 (2021): 1-22.

9. Flood, Andrew (Winter 1999). "The Zapatistas, anarchism and 'Direct democracy'". *Anarcho-Syndicalist Review*. 27.

10. Devaney, Laura et al. "Environmental Literacy and Deliberative Democracy: a Content Analysis of Written Submissions to the Irish Citizens' Assembly on Climate Change." *Climatic change* 162.4 (2020): 1965–1984. Web.

11. Extinction Rebellion

12. Ejsing, Mads, Adam Veng, and Irina Papazu. "Green Politics Beyond the State: Radicalizing the Democratic Potentials of Climate Citizens' Assemblies." *Climatic change* 176.6 (2023): 73–73. Web.

13. However, who can vote or even speak varies widely. For example, in Maine, if someone is not a town voter then they cannot speak unless two-thirds of the voters present agree that they may speak.

14. Please bear in mind that this argument about voice is not an argument about moral value: Animals and others are not worth more or less if they speak in more complex ways or if we have more extensive models of interaction. But the fact that other beings express their perspective on shared land, relations, and other topics, has democratic consequences. It means that, while humans sometimes have to speak for animals in order to bring to light their position in a world that does not listen to them, humans also need to speak *with* other animals in order to know how they feel, what they want, and how to work toward more just ways of living.

15. Adamatzky, Andrew. "Language of fungi derived from their electrical spiking activity." Royal Society Open Science 9.4 (2022): 211926.

16. *Multispecies Dialogues. Doing Philosophy with Animals, Children, the Sea and Others* (Amsterdam University Press, 2025: 35-36).

17. The position that we can never know for sure what goes on in the mind of someone else.

18. Donaldson, Sue, and Will Kymlicka. *Zoopolis: A political theory of animal rights*. Oxford University Press, USA, 2011.

19. Palmer, Clare. *Animal ethics in context*. Columbia University Press, 2010.

20. Celermajer, Danielle, et al. "Multispecies justice: theories, challenges, and a research agenda for environmental politics." *Trajectories in Environmental Politics* (2022): 116-137.Celermajer, Danielle, et al. "Justice through a multispecies lens." *Contemporary Political Theory* 19 (2020): 475-512.Celermajer, D., Schlosberg, D., Wadiwel, D., & Winter, C. (2023). A Political Theory for a Multispecies, Climate-Challenged World: 2050. *Political Theory*, 51(1), 39–53.

.

21. Wadiwel, Dinesh. *Animals and Capital*. Edinburgh University Press, 2023.

22. Winter, Christine J. "Unearthing the time/space/matter of multispecies justice." *Cultural Politics* 19.1 (2023): 39-56.

23. Latour, Bruno. 1993. *We Have Never Been Modern*. Cambridge, MA: Harvard University Press.

24. Latour uses the word 'actant' instead of 'actor' to emphasize that not only humans exercise agency. He describes the concept as follows: 'An "actor" in [actor-network theory] is a semiotic definition -an actant-, that is, something that acts or to which activity is granted by others. It implies no special motivation of human individual actors, nor of humans in general. An actant can literally be anything provided it is granted to be the source of an action.' http://www.bruno-latour.fr/sites/default/files/P-67%20ACTOR-NETWORK.pdf.

25. Biemann, Ursula, and Paulo Travers. 2020. *Forest law-Foresta giuridica*. Milan: nottetempo.

26. Espinosa, Cristina. "Interpretive affinities: The constitutionalization of rights of nature, Pacha Mama, in Ecuador." *Journal of Environmental Policy & Planning* 21.5 (2019): 608-622.

27. https://www.theguardian.com/world/2019/nov/30/saving-the-whanganui-can-personhood-rescue-a-river

28. Tănăsescu, Mihnea. "Rights of nature, legal personality, and indigenous philosophies." *Transnational environmental law* 9.3 (2020): 429-453.

29. Dinesh Wadiwel expresses this idea eloquently in *The War against Animals* (2015, Brill Publishers). In this book, Wadiwel shows that current understandings of 'rights' and 'property' are founded on violence towards nonhuman animals. Humans decided that the land and the other animals belonged to them, which is a claim of superiority, and not based on truth or a higher cosmic order, only on violence. Even the knowledge that humans have, and the institutions that are created to promote justice among humans, are based on a hierarchy in which humans dominate other animals. Rights can help to create different relations between humans and other animals, because they protect the vulnerable. But in thinking about the kinds of rights we need and about who decides what rights entail, we also need to zoom out, and challenge their history, in order not to repeat the violence and exclusion through which they were created.

30. Driessen, Clemens. *Animal deliberation: The co-evolution of technology and ethics on the farm*. Wageningen University and Research, 2014.

31. Meijer, Eva. *When animals speak: Toward an interspecies democracy*. NYU Press, 2019, Chapter 9.

32. Donaldson, Sue. "Animal agora: Animal citizens and the democratic challenge." *Social Theory and Practice* (2020): 709-735.

33. Plumwood, Val. Environmental Culture: The Ecological Crisis of Reason. New York; London: Routledge, 2002: 112.

34. In my work about animals and language (for example in *When Animals Speak*, 2019, New York University Press), I argue that Ludwig Wittgenstein's concept 'language-game' offers a good starting point for thinking about animal languages and interspecies language. Wittgenstein writes that we cannot give one definition of language. In the *Philosophical Investigations* (1958, Blackwell, translated by G.E.M. Anscombe), he shows that there are many different ways in which humans use language that are related but do not share one characteristic, and there is not one way to describe them. In studying language, we should not aim to find a definition, but rather map the different uses of language, which he calls language-games. He uses the term language-game in different ways: to refer to very simple forms of language use, but also to cover language as a whole, viewing it as consisting of many different language-games. Importantly, language-games involve not only speaking, but gestures, sounds, body language and other forms of communication too. While there are some language-games that take place only in the human realm, such as reading and writing novels, other animals also have their own language-games, and there are language-games that take place between animals of different species. Think for example of greeting: humans greet one another in many ways, by using the word 'hello', waving, hugging, looking someone in the eye or not. Mice can greet each other with a kiss, by twisting together their tails, or aligning their bodies. Humans and other animals also greet one another, by using words or other sounds, touch, nodding, looking at someone, and in many other ways.

35. Simpson, Leanne Betasamosake. *As we have always done: Indigenous freedom through radical resistance*. U of Minnesota Press, 2017.

36. Wall Kimmerer, Robin. *Braiding sweetgrass: Indigenous wisdom, scientific knowledge and the teachings of plants*. Milkweed editions, 2013.

37. Lawrence, Anna M. "Listening to plants: Conversations between critical plant studies and vegetal geography." *Progress in Human Geography* 46.2 (2022): 629-651.

38. Winter, Christine J. "Unearthing the time/space/matter of multispecies justice." *Cultural Politics* 19.1 (2023): 39-56.

39. See for example: Whiten, Andrew. "The burgeoning reach of animal culture." *Science* 372.6537 (2021): eabe6514 and Brakes, Philippa, et al. "A deepening understanding of animal culture suggests lessons for conservation." Proceedings of the Royal Society B 288.1949 (2021): 20202718.

40. Escobar, Arturo. *Pluriversal politics: The real and the possible*. Duke University Press, 2020.

41. jones, pattrice. *Bird's-Eye Views. Queer Queries About Activism, Animals, and Identity*. VINE Press, 2023.

42. Blattner, Charlotte E., Sue Donaldson, and Ryan Wilcox. "Animal agency in community." *Politics and Animals* 6.0 (2020): 1-22. See also jones, pattrice. *Bird's-Eye Views. Queer Queries About Activism, Animals, and Identity*. VINE Press, 2023.

43. Gillespie, Kathryn. *The cow with ear tag# 1389*. University of Chicago Press, 2020, p. 127.

44. Smuts, Barbara. "Encounters with animal minds." *Journal of consciousness studies* 8.5-6 (2001): 293-309.

45. Gruen, Lori. *Entangled Empathy: An Alternative Ethic for Our Relationships with Animals*. Lantern Publishing & Media, 2015.

46. See for example: Pellow, David Naguib. *Total liberation: The power and promise of animal rights and the radical earth movement*. U of Minnesota Press, 2014. See also: Colling, Sarat, Sean Parson, and Alessandro Arrigoni. "Until all are free: Total liberation through revolutionary decolonization, groundless solidarity, and a relationship framework." *Counterpoints* 448 (2014): 51-73.

47. Many projects that focus on political representation, inclusion and participation of the more-than-human world include art, such as the Embassy of the North Sea, Snæfellsjökul for president, and the More Than Human Life (MOTH) Project.

48. I discuss multispecies dialogues in more detail in *Multispecies Dialogues. Doing Philosophy with Animals, Children, the Sea and Others* (Amsterdam University Press, forthcoming).

49. Zwamborn, Miek. *The Seaweed Collector's Handbook: From Purple Laver to Peacock's Tail*. Profile Books, 2020.

50. Meijer, Eva. (2023). Deep Listening and Democracy: Political Listening to Fellow Citizens and Other Beings. *The Philosopher*, *111*(1), 53-60.

51. Slobodchikoff, Constantine Nicholas, Bianca S. Perla, and Jennifer L. Verdolin. *Prairie dogs: communication and community in an animal society*. Harvard University Press, 2009.

52. Janik, Vincent M., and Laela S. Sayigh. "Communication in bottlenose dolphins: 50 years of signature whistle research." *Journal of Comparative Physiology A* 199 (2013): 479-489.

53. Berg, Karl S., et al. "Vertical transmission of learned signatures in a wild parrot." *Proceedings of the Royal Society B: Biological Sciences* 279.1728 (2012): 585-591.

54. https://www.smithsonianmag.com/smart-news/researchers-translate-bat-talk-and-they-argue-lot-180961564/

55. Ten Cate, Carel. "Assessing the uniqueness of language: Animal grammatical abilities take center stage." *Psychonomic bulletin & review* 24.1 (2017): 91-96.

56. Byrne, R. A., et al. "Squid say it with skin: a graphic model for skin displays in Caribbean reef squid (Sepioteuthis sepioidea)." *Warnke K, Keupp H, Boletzky Sv (eds) Coleoid cephalopods through time. Berliner Paläobiol Abh* 3 (2003): 29-35.

57. Mejdell, Cecilie M., et al. "Horses can learn to use symbols to communicate their preferences." *Applied Animal Behaviour Science* 184 (2016): 66-73.

58. Yeon, Seong C., et al. "Differences between vocalization evoked by social stimuli in feral cats and house cats." *Behavioural processes* 87.2 (2011): 183-189.

59. Haraway, Donna Jeanne. *The companion species manifesto: Dogs, people, and significant otherness*. Vol. 1. Chicago: Prickly Paradigm Press, 2003.

60. Correia-Caeiro, Catia, Kun Guo, and Daniel S. Mills. "Perception of dynamic facial expressions of emotion between dogs and humans." *Animal cognition* 23.3 (2020): 465-476.

61. Nagasawa, Miho, et al. "Oxytocin-gaze positive loop and the coevolution of human-dog bonds." *Science* 348.6232 (2015): 333-336.

62. Gaita, Raimond. *The Philosopher's Dog*. Routledge, 2016.

63. An exception in political animal philosophy is the work of Sue Donaldson, see for example "Animal agora: Animal citizens and the democratic challenge." *Social Theory and Practice* (2020): 709-735.

64. For example, they scream when being cut. Khait, Itzhak, et al. "Sounds emitted by plants under stress are airborne and informative." Cell 186.7 (2023): 1328-1336.

65. See for example: Gaard, Greta. *Critical ecofeminism*. Lexington Books, 2017.

66. Wall Kimmerer, Robin. *Braiding sweetgrass: Indigenous wisdom, scientific knowledge and the teachings of plants*. Milkweed editions, 2013.

67. Wall, John. *Children's rights: Today's global challenge*. Rowman & Littlefield, 2016.

68. See: Holmberg, Arita, and Aida Alvinius. "Children's protest in relation to the climate emergency: A qualitative study on a new form of resistance promoting political and social change." *Childhood* 27.1 (2020): 78-92. and: Nissen, Sylvia, Jennifer HK Wong, and Sally Carlton. "Children and young people's climate crisis activism–a perspective on long-term effects." *Children's Geographies* 19.3 (2021): 317-323. See also: Sanz-Caballero, Susana. "Children's rights in a changing climate: a perspective from the United Nations Convention on the Rights of the Child." *Ethics in science and environmental politics* 13.1 (2013): 1-14.

69. Christou, Georgina. *Children Out of Place with Childhood: Pupils' Assemblies, Direct Action, Serious Play and Public Space in Youth's Autonomous Horizontal Politics in Cyprus*. Diss. University of Sussex, 2018.

70. McGuire, Luke, Sally B. Palmer, and Nadira S. Faber. "The development of speciesism: Age-related differences in the moral view of animals." *Social Psychological and Personality Science* 14.2 (2023): 228-237.

71. Sheldrake, Merlin. *Entangled life: How fungi make our worlds, change our minds & shape our futures*. Random House Trade Paperbacks, 2021.

72. Winter, Christine J., and David Schlosberg. "What matter matters as a matter of justice?." *Environmental Politics* (2023): 1-20.

73. Natura 2000 is a European netwerk of protected nature reserves.

74. I discuss this case study in detail in Meijer, E. (2023). Speaking about Farming: Embodied Deliberation and Resistance of Cows and Farmers in the Netherlands. In J. Dugnoille, & E. Vander Meer (Eds.), *Animals Matter: Resistance and Transformation in Animal Commodification* (pp. 132-154). (Human-Animal Studies; Vol. 26). Brill.

75. I borrow this model from Stichting Kapitaloceen, a Dutch anti-capitalist and anti-speciesist farming cooperation that already works in this way. See www.kapitaloceen.nl.

76. Srinivasan, Krithika. "Re-animalising wellbeing: Multispecies justice after development." *The Sociological Review* 70.2 (2022): 352-366.

77. Ko, Aph, and Syl Ko. *Aphro-ism: Essays on pop culture, feminism, and black veganism from two sisters*. Lantern Publishing & Media, 2017.

78. Wohlleben, Peter. *The hidden life of trees: What they feel, how they communicate—Discoveries from a secret world*. Vol. 1. Greystone Books, 2016.

79. Zwamborn, Miek. *The Seaweed Collector's Handbook: From Purple Laver to Peacock's Tail*. Profile Books, 2020.

80. Celermajer, Danielle. *Summertime. Reflections on a vanishing future*. Hamish Hamilton, 2021.

81. Meijer, Eva. "Developing multispecies education with children and animals." *On Education. Journal for Research and Debate* 6.16 (2023).

ACKNOWLEDGMENTS

First of all, I would like to thank pattrice jones, whose careful and insightful editorial remarks greatly helped improve this essay. I also want to thank pattrice and the other people at VINE Press for their enthusiasm and trust in this text. Thanks to Hallie Abelman and Jetske Brouwer for their questions and remarks too. My ideas are co-shaped by the nonhuman beings with whom I share my life, most notably Doris, Olli, Klontje, Kruidje, and Simba, as well as the garden and its inhabitants. Without them, my work would not exist.

www.ingramcontent.com/pod-product-compliance
Lightning Source LLC
Chambersburg PA
CBHW070643030426
42337CB00020B/4143